The Future of Banking

The Future of Banking

James L. Pierce

Foreword by Richard C. Leone

A Twentieth Century Fund Report
Yale University Press
New Haven and London

Designed by Sylvia Steiner.
Set in Garamond Book type by The Composing Room of Michigan,
Grand Rapids, Michigan.
Printed in the United States of America by Vail-Ballou Press, Binghamton,
New York.

Library of Congress Cataloging-in-Publication Data

Pierce, James L.
The future of banking / James L. Pierce ; foreword by Richard C. Leone.
    p. cm.
    "A Twentieth Century Fund report."
    Includes bibliographical references and index.
    ISBN 0-300-05058-5
    1. Banks and banking—United States.   2. Banking law—United
States.   I. Title.
HG2491.P54   1991
332.1'0973—dc20   91-158 CIP

10   9   8   7   6   5   4   3   2   1

Contents

Foreword

Americans who think about public policy or even make it are by and large not economists or otherwise experts on the financial system. Yet, in the wake of the collapse of the thrift industry, they are raising serious questions concerning the soundness and even the role of the nation's commercial banks. Long before those concerns reached their current intensity, the Twentieth Century Fund asked James L. Pierce of the University of California, Berkeley, a distinguished economist and expert on the banking system, to look at the future of banking in the United States. We also asked him to make his assessment of the situation accessible to an audience of nonexperts. He has fulfilled that mission at a time when the breadth and interest of such an audience is greater than it has been at any time since the Great Depression.

Pierce's analysis moves beyond the media focus on the failing network of thrifts to consider the implications of an increasing number of commercial bank failures, some of them quite large, over the past decade. He traces the history of these developments and looks back to their antecedents earlier in the century. He believes that a major cause for the present uncertainty about the banking system lies in an ineffective and inappropriate mix of regulation and deregulation—a set of rules and exemptions premised upon the sort of financial world we lived in during the 1930s. His forecast for the future of American banking assumes that the policy choices made in Washington will play the crucial role.

Pierce presents an argument for fundamental change built upon a belief that an alteration of such magnitude is inevitable. Some of his solutions are novel. All are provocative. But few would assert that the distinction he draws between the monetary and nonmonetary functions of the institutions we call banks is not the essential analytical basis for conducting a reasoned debate about future policy.

The 1990s are likely to be a time when America reexamines in a fairly fundamental way the question of what is the proper mix of regulation and deregulation in our version of capitalism. Getting the mix just right may well be impossible. This book, however, certainly moves us along the path toward better understanding at least of what we should be considering in one central area of economic activity. It is in the best tradition of Twentieth Century Fund works, analyzing a problem insightfully and then dealing boldly with the policy implications of that analysis.

We thank James Pierce for bringing his long experience and sharp intellect to this task for us. The result of his thinking should make a substantial contribution to the ongoing debate about the future of banking in the United States.

Richard C. Leone, *Director*
The Twentieth Century Fund
February 1991

Acknowledgments

When the Twentieth Century Fund approached me to write about the future of banking, they asked for a book that would be accessible to more than economists and other specialists alone. Although I concurred that such a volume was needed, I underestimated the difficulty in producing it. It is hard for an economist, and an academic one at that, to forgo the jargon, streams of numbers, statistical analysis, scholarly footnotes with endless references, and other baggage of the discipline while still presenting a rigorous argument. But I hope the effort has succeeded—there is a pressing need for a wide audience to understand that banking and its regulation must be reformed if the nation is to continue to prosper and avoid financial instability. These issues are too important to be left to specialists. But the research of specialists has been crucial in providing the theoretical and empirical foundation for this book. I do not intend to slight these researchers by the absence of extensive footnote citations, simply to spare general readers wear and tear. The selected references provided at the end of the book should make up, in part, for the lack of extensive citations of the literature.

As with any undertaking like this, there are many people to thank. I am grateful to the Twentieth Century Fund for its gracious and generous support not only in finances but also in the patience exercised by

Beverly Goldberg and others when substantial delays arose in completing the book. I am also grateful to Samuel Chase for our many conversations concerning numerous topics covered in this book. His critical comments and editorial advice have been invaluable. Roger Craine, William Dudley, Edward Ettin, Thomas Havrilesky, Robert Litan, Thomas Thomson, and Donald Tucker have also generously given me their expert views and comments. Peter Sheats, Susan Pierce, and Jonathan Pierce reviewed the manuscript with great care, providing many useful comments from the perspective of nonspecialists. I am also indebted to an anonymous reviewer retained by Yale University Press whose comments induced me to tighten and sharpen the discussion at several points. Alex Holzman and Steven Greenfield helpfully served as formal editors from the Twentieth Century Fund, and at Yale University Press Laura Jones Dooley provided excellent editorial services and John Covell orchestrated publication on a short deadline. The book simply could not have been completed without the dedicated work of Suzanne Edwards, who provided able research and editorial assistance and who miraculously transformed my handwritten drafts into a manuscript. Finally, I thank my son Sam for showing so much patience and understanding concerning the time I spent with this project rather than with him.

The Future of Banking

1

Does Banking Have a Future?

The public hears a seemingly unrelenting barrage of bad news about banking. Citibank, Chase Manhattan, Morgan Guaranty, and other giants write off as worthless billions of dollars of loans to Latin America, but the problem does not go away; defaults on low-grade corporate bonds raise concerns that the massive amount of bank lending to support corporate takeovers (leveraged buyouts) will be the next threat; and just as defaults on real estate loans in the energy-producing states finally begin to abate, defaults accelerate sharply in Arizona and in the Northeast. Large banks are no longer pillars of stability: Continental Illinois of Chicago, one of the nation's largest banks, collapses and is taken over by the government; First Republic Bancorp and MCorp of Dallas, First City Bancorp of Houston, First Pennsylvania, and the Bank of New England all fail and require massive federal assistance; Bank of America loses its place as the nation's largest and most stable bank, staggering from one crisis to another before finally returning to profitability. Even Citibank, now our largest bank, suffers huge losses and embarks on a program of retrenchment. Small banks vanish at an alarming rate as each year through 1989 establishes a new record for the number of bank failures experienced since the Great Depression. In 1988 the Federal Deposit Insurance Corporation (FDIC), the agency that insures bank deposits, registers its first operating loss in its fifty-five-year history as it struggles to cope with over two hundred bank failures; and it sustains additional losses in the years that follow. At the same time, the FDIC assumes new burdens when it takes over duties for insuring savings and loan associations, whose own insurance agency (the Federal Savings and Loan Insurance Corporation, FSLIC) has gone bankrupt. In 1989, the government moves to stop hemorrhaging in the thrift industry—savings and loans, and savings banks, which have powers similar to those of banks—engaging in an expensive bailout of their insurance and revamping their regulation. But thrifts continue to fail and the taxpayer expense of bailing out their bankrupt insurance fund skyrockets. Meanwhile, concerns begin to surface that the FDIC's bank insurance fund could go broke, subjecting taxpayers to even greater burden.

The banking and thrift industries are highly protected and regulated precisely to prevent these problems from occurring. What has gone wrong with government regulation and deposit insurance, and how can the situation be corrected? The answers to these and related questions are varied, but in the most basic terms, the financial world has changed fundamentally while the government's approach to bank and thrift regulation, and to deposit insurance, has not. The approach worked fine when it was put in place nearly sixty years ago, but it is badly out of step with the highly integrated and rapidly moving financial environment made possible today by the revolutions in computer and telecommunications technologies. The government's approach to regulation and deposit insurance must be brought into compatibility with the times. If it is not, the situation will not improve appreciably, and it could worsen.

Although the current problems are serious and deep-seated, there is yet time to act in an orderly and thoughtful manner. In spite of the unfavorable publicity and all the problems, both self-inflicted and external, most banks and many thrifts are still functioning well. There is no imminent danger of collapse. Yes, banking has a future, but how bright that future is depends crucially on the nature and degree of change that occurs in governmental policies concerning bank regulation and deposit insurance. Banking's ailments will not disappear by themselves.

Banking has changed and continues to change in ways that are fundamentally altering its role within the nation's financial system. Banks are no longer simply passive gatherers of local deposits and dispensers of loans to local business. Many are huge multinational corporations competing for funds in markets throughout the world while providing a host of financial services both across the country and overseas. These services include not only every kind of loan imaginable but also forms of investment banking, insurance, stock and bond brokerage, leasing, and loan "securitization." Their ability to engage in underwriting and other securities activities is particularly great abroad because of an absence of regulatory restrictions. Smaller banks usually operate only at home, but they, too, compete actively for funds, offer an increasing assortment of financial services, and participate in international loans originated by larger banks. Even the hallowed prohibition against interstate branching has broken down, with many banks forming regional and even national networks. And as bankers have entered new markets, their turf has been invaded by a multitude of nonbanking competitors offering traditional banking services. These changes have produced grave problems for bank regulation, which has not adapted to this radically different financial environment.

This book is about banking's problems and how they can be solved. Its purpose is not to alarm or to point an accusing finger at guilty parties. Rather, it looks at the basic economic, technological, and regulatory factors that have brought banking to the present and will determine its future direction. I propose fundamental changes in banking powers, deposit insurance, and bank regulation; if adopted, they will allow the financial services industry to meet the nation's needs for many years to come. In spite of the huge difficulties that the thrift industry faces, my emphasis is on commercial banks, for it is the banks that play a dominant role in the nation's monetary system and are a crucial source of credit for many businesses. But the proposals are intended ultimately to apply to thrifts as well, and where relevant the thrift industry is discussed directly.

Most proposals to reform banking attack symptoms and not disease. If banks have lent too much money to Brazil, Mexico, or other developing nations, then require them to lend less. If banks have insufficient capital, make them have more. If banks are assuming too much risk, force them to take on less. The presumption behind reactions like these is that banks are in trouble because they have not been behaving themselves. Like errant children, they must be disciplined and their behavior constrained.

Although there are some conspicuous examples of undisciplined and mismanaged banks, most are well managed; the problems are not so superficial. Fundamentally, banking and the government programs that condition the industry are becoming incompatible with the integrated, high-technology financial world in which we live. This fact is central to banking's future success.

The sophistication and complexity of modern banks mask the fact that the structure of the industry was determined largely by the New Deal banking legislation of the 1930s, which was intended to end the financial panics and banking collapses that had plagued the nation since its inception. In pursuing these objectives, legislation established a regulatory environment for banking that has prevailed to this day. Passed in a crisis atmosphere following collapse of the banking system and temporary closure of banks by President Franklin D. Roosevelt in 1933, the legislation employed many approaches, apparently on the premise that at least one would surely succeed in stablizing the banking system. The shotgun approach was understandable under the circumstances, and some elements did address and correct basic defects producing instability. But other elements involved "reforms" that treated symptoms, not disease, and created a government-designed structure for banking that has become increasingly removed from economic reality. These parts of the New Deal approach are sources of banking's current difficulties and should be changed.

The fundamental bank reform of the New Deal was to spread a federal "safety net" under the fractional-reserve banking system to eliminate bank runs and liquidity crises that could bring the system down. Under the fractional-reserve system, which remains in operation, banks accepted deposits that were payable on demand, set aside reserves to meet normal withdrawals, and used the rest of the funds to grant illiquid loans. This fractional-reserve arrangement worked fine as long as the public retained faith in banks. But if confidence were shaken, people would withdraw their money and hold cash instead. Bank runs, during which depositors tried to withdraw their money before the bank ran out, could and did develop. If these flights to currency were sufficiently sizable and widespread, reserves would be insufficient to cover them and banks would be unable to honor their commitment to allow withdrawals on demand—the money ran out. Bank runs could collapse the banking system, as they did in 1933.

The New Deal reforms solved the instability of the fractional-reserve system by instituting federal deposit insurance, which guaranteed insured depositors that their funds were safe. Legislation also reformed the Federal Reserve, converting it into an effective central bank that makes currency and reserves available to banks should runs occur. Deposit insurance and an effective Federal Reserve constituted a federal safety net that ended banking collapses. This safety net has been highly successful, but it is showing signs of wear and tear in today's rapidly changing financial environment.

The New Deal legislation did not stop there, however. The New Dealers also sought to make virtually every bank in the industry failure proof. They sought to accomplish this by isolating banks from the rest of the financial system and by assuring their profitability.

Neither goal could be successful in the long run. Isolation was accomplished in part by making banks stick to banking—the collection of deposits and dispensation of loans—or at least to activities closely related to ordinary banking. They were forced to abandon their corporate securities underwriting and other activities that the government perceived to be unrelated to banking and important sources of insolvency. In effect, banks were to be so tightly constrained that they could not stray into areas that could get them into trouble.

But there were and are, of course, plenty of opportunities to get into trouble performing ordinary banking, a problem the government addressed by trying to impose regulatory and supervisory standards so strict as to make it unlikely that a bank would get into difficulties. These standards seemed to be successful at least until the 1960s, but recent events have shown that they are increasingly difficult to impose.

The government lightened its regulatory burdens by pursuing policies to promote bank profitability. This was accomplished by limiting competition both from financial firms outside of banking and among banks themselves. Checking accounts were reserved exclusively for banks, and only banks had access to loans from the Federal Reserve and to its check-clearing facilities. Only banks and thrift institutions could offer federally insured deposit accounts of any kind. To protect the profitability of existing banks, entry of new banks into the industry was restricted, and competition among banks for the public's deposits was limited by prohibiting banks from paying interest on demand deposit balances—the only kind of checking account at the time—and by imposing ceilings on the interest rates banks could pay on other accounts. Again, these and other methods of isolating banks and promoting their profitability were successful for many years. Short of fraud, it was very difficult for a bank to fail.

Beginning in the late 1960s, economic and technological developments conspired to erode the barriers erected by New Deal legislation to isolate and protect banks. The result has been increasing the integration of banks with financial markets and the provision of many banklike services by nonbanking institutions. Banks have responded by seeking out new activities, but their efforts have often been thwarted by the requirement that they stick to banking, with the consequence that bank risk has risen while profitability has declined. In spite of the frustration over the legal barriers that prevent banks from entering various new areas, the lines between banks and other financial institutions have become blurred. Little about banking remains unique.

Swings in inflation and interest rates from the 1960s onward made it impossible to isolate bank deposit accounts from other financial investments. Although ceilings on deposit interest rates limited competition among banks, they did not shelter banks from the competition of the market. United States Treasury bills and other money market instruments are close substitutes for the bank accounts of major corporations, state and local governments, and wealthy individuals. These depositors were both willing and able to shift funds between banks and market securities in search of a high return.

Though large depositors could easily shift back and forth between bank accounts and money market instruments, for a time small depositors could not. But economic forces soon produced a new kind of institution that provided many small depositors with the ability to seek out attractive returns. When market interest rates soared in the 1970s, money market mutual funds were formed that allowed small savers, who lack direct access to the money market, to earn a high return. These money market funds pool the resources of many individuals to purchase short-term government securities, high-grade commercial paper (short-term, unsecured corporate debt), and banks' negotiable certificates of deposit (CDs), passing the return on to their customers. The accounts offered by money market funds are perfectly liquid. They are redeemable on demand; checks can be written against them to third parties, and wire transfers are available. Money market funds offered the same services as bank checking accounts, but, unlike the accounts at banks in the 1970s, they paid a market interest rate. With the development of money market funds, firms outside of banking found a way to take away banks' monopoly on checking accounts while offering the public a market rate of return. Computer and communication technology permitted this advance by enabling money market funds to provide their services at low cost, and high interest rates were the trigger. The result was a massive loss of funds by banks and thrifts.

Government-imposed ceilings on the interest rates that banks could pay kept their interest costs down when market interest rates rose, but they lost deposits. This fact of economic life eventually led to deregulation of most deposit interest rates in the 1980s, demonstrating that one of the premises of the New Deal approach was fundamentally unsound. Bank accounts are not so unusual that depositors are indifferent to the returns available from putting their funds to alternative use. These accounts cannot be isolated from the rest of the financial environment.

While the deregulation of deposit interest rates in the early 1980s blunted the attack of the money market funds, they continue to thrive. Banks' primary advantage over them is that money market funds do not enjoy federal insurance.[1] But unlike banks, which back their liabilities with relatively illiquid and risky loans, money market funds are backed by highly liquid, low-risk market securities. When it comes to offering a safe and liquid "deposit" account that pays a market rate of return, the funds simply have a superior product.

Banks have labored to integrate themselves with financial markets. They have become highly successful in tapping financial markets for vast amounts of funds. Large banks are no longer simply depositories where local households, businesses, and governments place their money. These "core" deposits still exist, but their importance has been superseded by hundreds of billions of dollars that the banks raise each year in the domestic and international money markets. Banks' negotiable certificates of deposit, Eurodollar deposits, and other obligations are deposits in name only. In reality, large banks issue tremendous amounts of short-term, highly liquid money market debt in world markets, directly competing with the short-term debt issued by governments and multinational firms. Today, large banks finance most of their operations with these debt instruments rather than with core deposits. It was the inevitable consequence of banks' desire to have more funds than their local depositors would provide and of the technology that allowed their money market instruments to be marketed on competitive terms. This is not the kind of deposit-taking banking that the New Deal reforms attempted to isolate and protect.

Money market instruments issued by large banks are commonly called managed liabilities to indicate that banks can quickly and easily manage the amounts outstanding (at least during good times). The rapid growth of liability management is an excellent example of how economic forces interact with high technology to produce integration of banks with financial markets. When market interest rates rose above ceiling rates on ordinary deposits in the later 1960s, the large banks that experienced deposit outflows responded by raising funds in the money

1. Money market funds have the advantage of not being subjected to noninterest-bearing reserve requirements, as are banks.

markets. Rapid development of liability management was possible because of advances in computer and telecommunications technology that substantially lowered the costs of these activities. Once in place, the "funds management" activities of large banks became integrated with and affected by financial conditions throughout the world. These banks became aggressive participants in the world's money markets. A combination of economic incentive and technological capability took large banks out of the niche carved for them by the New Deal legislation and plunked them right in the middle of some of the toughest and most unforgiving markets in the world. Deregulation of deposit interest rates in the early 1980s enabled many smaller institutions to enter the fray.

Managed liabilities provide large banks with tremendous flexibility, but they also offer a temptation for expansion that has been too great for many to resist. The enormous growth in loans to LDCs (less developed countries), energy firms, and real estate developers in the 1970s and early 1980s was financed mainly by managed liabilities. Tapping world money markets for funds, bank lending grew rapidly during the 1970s, making banks increasingly vulnerable to loan losses. Two of the largest banking failures following the New Deal reforms—Franklin National in 1974 and Continental Illinois in 1985—were caused in large part by too rapid expansion supported by managed liabilities.

Large banks are multinational firms that support the bulk of their operations not with your or my deposits but with funds raised in the world's money markets. Many smaller banks and thrifts are active in the national market for funds, which is facilitated by deposit brokers, who collect money from customers looking for high returns and deliver it to institutions willing to pay the price. When it comes to deposits and other liabilities, the attempts of the New Deal reforms to separate banking from other financial markets have failed.

Financial markets have impinged on banks not only from the deposit side but also from the lending side. Banks were traditionally the source of short-term loans to big business. After banks experienced deposit losses in the second half of the 1960s and had difficulty meeting their lending commitments, many large businesses lost faith in banks as reliable sources of short-term credit. Big business found that it did not have to rely on banks after all. Advances in computer and telecommunications technology allowed large firms to raise funds reliably at low cost in the commercial paper market. Today, banks are not the major source of conventional short-term loans to many big businesses; they use the commercial paper market instead. This exodus of major business from banks as a source of credit was a major blow, inducing banks to seek out such new borrowers as smaller domestic companies and LDCs abroad and to search for such new activities as investment banking overseas and financing corporate takeovers at home.

Banking's problems have been compounded by the growth of non-bank financial conglomerates that provide many attractive services to the public. These conglomerates offer money market funds, stock and bond funds, securities brokerage services, real estate brokerage and finance, insurance, and many other financial services in one institution. They engage in the equivalent of deposit banking while offering in some respects a wider range of other financial services than banks are allowed to provide. Financial conglomerates are operated not only by such conventional financial firms such as Merrill Lynch and American Express, but also by such retailers as Sears and such manufacturers as General Motors, General Electric, and Ford. The financial conglomerates have broken down the barriers to banking in a major way. They can even offer conventional banking services through ownership of a thrift institution. Banking's preserve has been invaded; there is simply nothing unique about banking any longer.

Rather than enjoying the competitive advantages initially provided in the New Deal legislation, banks are placed at a competitive disadvantage by economic, technological, and financial developments. The financial conglomerates are subject to much less regulation than banks, yet they provide many banking services. Growth of the financial conglomerates amply illustrates why there must be regulation by function rather than regulation by type of legally defined entity.

Banking and its government regulators are not in tune with the highly integrated, high-technology world in which we live. The New Deal approach is simply inappropriate and unworkable in the modern financial environment. Nonbanks can find ways to offer profitable banking services, and bankers will try to find ways to enter profitable new lines of business. The banking regulators have been unwilling to accept this economic fact and have instead tried to preserve an outdated system that keeps banks in "banking" and nonbanks out. They have not succeeded, but they have unwittingly encouraged undue risk taking by banks striving to find profitable lines of activity within their limited confines. The adverse results are only too visible.

In the 1980s, regulators had no choice but to eliminate interest rate ceilings for most deposit accounts; competition from securities markets and money market funds would have drained banks and thrifts dry had the rate ceilings remained in place. The deregulation that occurred was a belated recognition of what had become painfully obvious: unless depository institutions are competitive, people will take their business elsewhere.

Much noise has been made in the press about how interest rate deregulation caused so many bank failures. In reality, relatively few bank failures resulted from decontrolling deposit interest rates. Following the New Deal reforms, in every year before 1984, most bank failures resulted from fraud, an evil practice that certainly predates decontrol of deposit interest rates. Beginning in 1980, the number of failures unrelated to fraud began increasing, and by 1984 fraud was no longer the primary cause of failures. This coincidence with deregulation is not necessarily a cause. In fact, the rise in failures resulted primarily from a devastating recession and a set of circumstances that had ruinous effects on banks with heavy concentrations of loans in real estate, energy, agriculture, and LDCs, all incurred *before* deregulation.

There have, of course, been instances where the necessity of paying higher interest rates on accounts eroded bank earnings and cases where increased deposit costs weakened already feeble institutions and tipped them into failure. Some banks tried to grow their way out of adversity by using managed liabilities or brokered deposits to finance expansion. Their rapid growth, unaccompanied by additional equity capital or regulatory discipline, exposed these institutions to increased risk, and many did not make it. Still, it is a mistake to lay the blame for the large increase in bank failures on the doorstep of deposit interest rate deregulation.

Deregulation played a larger role in the increasing failures of savings and loan associations and other thrifts. At the same time that deposit interest rate ceilings were deregulated for thrifts, they also received substantial new investment powers. Once almost totally reliant on mortgage lending, thrifts could now enter not only into such banklike areas as consumer and business loans but also into risky avenues like real estate development and low-grade commercial bonds (junk bonds) that are prohibited for banks. Presented with such seemingly juicy opportunities, the temptation to cast off prudence was too great for some thrifts. Nor were their regulators up to the task of limiting the risk taking in which many engaged; the results were disastrous. With about a third of the industry insolvent or nearly so, and with the FSLIC bankrupt, the government launched an expensive program to recapitalize the thrifts' insurance fund, putting it under the FDIC.

The problems of many thrifts were thus exacerbated by the deregulation of deposit interest rates; they were able to raise large amounts of funds by paying high interest rates on their insured accounts, using deposit brokers to deliver funds collected from investors all over the country. Access to these funds allowed many thrifts that were tottering on the edge of bankruptcy to gamble on risky ventures. They had little to lose and much to gain if fortune smiled on them. When the ventures did not pan out, the thrift insurance agency, the FSLIC, was stuck with the losses. Thrift regulators did not control the risk-seeking behavior of many of their wards, prompting the government to revamp thrift regulation in 1989.

The behavior of the FDIC, which insures bank deposits, and the Federal Reserve, which provides "emergency" loans to banks, has also contributed, albeit indirectly and unwittingly, to greater risk taking by banks and to the increasing rate of bank failure. When a bank fails, the FDIC typically does not close it down and pay off insured depositors; instead, the insurance agency finds another bank to purchase the failed one. Before a purchaser can be found, large, uninsured depositors often withdraw their funds, and the Federal Reserve keeps the bank afloat by providing loans to replace those lost to withdrawals. When a purchaser is finally found, the acquiring bank buys the failed bank's assets and assumes its deposit liabilities, including those to remaining uninsured depositors. This allows the newly reorganized bank to continue in operation—a convenience to its customers—and it tends to reduce the cost to the government's insurance fund, at least in the short run. But by arranging assumptions of all deposit liabilities of failed banks, the FDIC, with the help of the Federal Reserve, ends up protecting all the bank's depositors, including holders of negotiable CDs and Eurodeposits, not simply insured depositors. With all depositors protected, large, uninsured depositors have little incentive to provide market discipline by insisting on premium interest rates or withdrawing funds if a bank appears too risky. With the incentive of uninsured depositors blunted, more of the burden of controlling bank risk taking falls on regulators. Bank regulators have often been unable to perform this difficult task, which accounts partly for the increase in bank failures, just as it did for thrifts.

In the current environment, it may be tempting to try to turn the clock back to an earlier, simpler time by severely restricting what banks can do. Such efforts are unlikely to succeed, but even if they did, many monetary and financial activities currently conducted by banks would simply be shifted to less regulated elements of the financial system. Banks would lose and the new financial conglomerates would gain, with little prospect for enhancing monetary and financial stability. Trying to turn back the clock would not reverse the reality that with each new financial innovation and electronic marvel, the financial system becomes more integrated.

The Need for Fundamental Changes in Bank Regulation

Although the financial picture has changed greatly, the social objectives of avoiding monetary and financial instability and achieving an efficient allocation of credit are as valid today as they ever were. These objectives are becoming increasingly difficult to achieve within the existing regulatory environment. To ensure their attainment in the future requires a fundamentally different approach. Banking and its regulatory regime must be reformed in ways that are perhaps as far-reaching as those adopted during the New Deal. Earlier reforms had to await a financial collapse; this time needed changes can occur without such a catalyst.

This book argues for a fundamental change in the way banking is viewed, regulated, and insured. Its basic message is that if financial stability is to be maintained and banks are to have a future, forced financial specialization must end. It is no longer possible or even desirable to bequeath certain financial activities to banks and exclude others from offering them. What specialization occurs should be the result of economic forces, not a consequence of government edict. The economic forces of the marketplace will ensure that the services currently supplied by banks are provided at low cost.

The government does have the absolutely essential role of ensuring that monetary and financial stability are maintained, but its safety net has to be adapted to the modern world. Stability does *not* require that most banking activities be isolated and protected; most of what banks currently do can be safely integrated with other parts of the financial system. Stability does require viable deposit insurance and a strong central bank, and these fundamental governmental elements must be part of the financial system of the future.

The proposed reforms can be stated rather simply. The basic idea is to design a regulatory system around financial functions rather than around the type of institution that happens to provide them. This has traditionally come down to regulating banks because banks performed monetary and loan functions that were vital to the nation's financial health. Banks offered monetary accounts (accounts payable on demand), using the funds deposited to finance their lending.

All of this has changed now, but the regulatory structure has not. Banks are no longer the sole supplier of deposits payable on demand; money market funds and similar institutions provide much the same service. And, while banks remain an important source of credit to business, there are many other lenders as well. The commercial paper and bond markets take care of most of the credit needs of large businesses. Insurance companies, pension funds, venture capitalists, factoring and commercial-credit companies, and providers of trade credit offer important sources of credit to medium-size and small businesses. Finally, the banking industry has changed tremendously in the way that it finances loans. Demand obligations are no longer the primary means of funding loans. Conventional time accounts, negotiable CDs, Eurodollars, and other liabilities are now the primary sources of bank funds.

These changes have two important implications. First, because monetary services are no longer a bank monopoly, federal insurance should be available to all institutions that offer checking accounts and payments services, provided they are subjected to strict and uniform regulation. This principle applies regardless of whether the institution offering monetary services happens to be a bank, a thrift, Merrill Lynch, Sears, or General Motors. Furthermore, the checking accounts and payments services offered by these institutions should have federal insurance no matter what the size of the account or payment. Second, given that checking accounts supply proportionally ever less of the funds used for bank loans, concerns over the safety of these accounts can be separated from concerns over the quality of bank lending. For regulatory purposes, monetary functions can be separated from conventional lending functions even though both are available within a bank. This allows a tremendous simplification in the way the banks are regulated. Separation is the cornerstone of the reform proposal.

Under the proposal, banks as they exist today are legally separated into two parts: a monetary part and everything else. The monetary function is tightly regulated and completely insured by the federal government. All other functions are outside the jurisdiction of the banking regulators, and all government insurance and guarantees are eliminated for the time accounts and other liabilities used to finance various activities. The division between monetary and nonmonetary functions is accomplished by requiring that any bank or other institution offering insured checking accounts and payment services maintain a monetary service company within it, which is a separate corporation only engaging in these activities. This monetary service company is operated in much the same way as money market funds are operated today, but it has an equity position financed by stockholders. The company provides checking accounts and invests the funds in high-grade, short-term money market instruments such as Treasury bills, commercial paper, and short-term instruments issued by providers of nonmonetary financial services. Strict regulations are applied concerning both the securities that are eligible to back insured checking accounts and the minimum degree of diversification of investments that is required. Essentially, the same rules that guide existing money market funds apply. Any existing bank, money market fund, or other entity that wants to offer federally insured checking accounts can put up the required capital and form a monetary service company, provided it plays by the rules. Entry of new firms into the monetary service industry is open to any who qualify. An institution offering insured checking accounts can also provide payment services, handling payments to third parties by check or wire transfer. These are also strictly supervised, regulated, and insured to ensure the integrity of the payments system.

This simple approach provides a degree of safety for checking accounts and the payments system that is impossible to achieve when checking accounts are backed by bank loans and other activities. It is essential to realize, however, that converting the monetary part of banking into monetary service companies does not eliminate the possibility of panics and liquidity crises should the public lose faith. The chances of such events occurring are reduced markedly but not eliminated. News of an employee running off to Rio with all the money or of the failure of a large borrower in the commercial paper market could trigger depositor panic at solvent monetary service companies. Here, only the federal government can come to the rescue. A federal safety net must support the nation's monetary system. Immediate payoff of all depositors from a failed monetary service company must occur, and the Federal Reserve must step in to provide whatever liquidity is required of solvent institutions to stop a crisis. These facets of the New Deal reforms are retained and used whenever necessary.

This covers the monetary side of banking, but what about the rest? Here the approach is very different. Banks and anyone else are free to issue uninsured liabilities and grant loans to their hearts' content, provided that these activities are conducted through companies that are separate from their monetary service companies. The monetary and nonmonetary functions can have common ownership and be part of a bank or financial conglomerate—they can even occupy the same location and share personnel and information—but the monetary service company can have no financial dealings with other companies under common ownership. Failure of a nonmonetary company will have no effect on the safety and soundness of the monetary service company.

Institutions that offer traditional banking services will look much like the banks of today, with tellers and loan officers. Customers using checking accounts—the liabilities of the institutions' monetary service companies—have government insurance protection. Customers choosing other kinds of accounts, such as CDs, have no protection; these accounts are liabilities of institutions' nonmonetary companies, which receive absolutely no federal insurance and no guarantees of safety. Holders of these liabilities will be clearly informed that their funds are at risk. These customers have a powerful incentive to provide needed discipline by insisting on adequate capital, by imposing premiums for risk, and ultimately by taking their business elsewhere if the issuers of the liabilities are assuming too much risk. Market discipline replaces heavy-handed and often ineffectual governmental risk regulation. For reasons described in a later chapter, market discipline will reduce the chances of a liquidity scramble of the sort that surrounded the Continental Illinois affair. Should such a scramble occur, however, the Federal Reserve is available to provide the needed liquidity to the market. Monetary service companies aid in the process by acting as conduits for loans from the Federal Reserve.

When matters are set up as proposed, there is no reason to distinguish between banks and other types of financial firms. Anyone can enter the monetary service field and anyone can perform nonmonetary functions, but the financial affairs of the two activities must be kept separate. The distinction between banks and nonbanks simply disappears. Banks can expand into full financial service firms that offer a wide variety of services; in effect, they join the financial conglomerates in becoming the supermarkets of finance. All parties have to abide by the same rules and are regulated alike. Bank regulation in its current form ceases. It is replaced by tough, streamlined regulation of monetary service companies.

In arguing for this proposal, it is necessary to answer many questions. How does the government's safety net operate and will it be effective? Can the monetary functions of banks be effectively separated from all their other activities or will banks find ways to undercut the separation? What are the implications for the volume of credit extended by what are now banks if their nonmonetary liabilities are no longer insured or guaranteed? What are the implications for small banks and the loans they now grant? What are the implications for the international competitiveness of large banks if their nonmonetary accounts are no longer protected? What happens if banks are allowed into securities underwriting, general insurance, and other financial activities, areas now closed to them? What happens to thrifts? Can monetary policy be effective if the monetary side of banking becomes the near equivalent of a money market fund? Is it possible to have an orderly transition to the proposed regime? Answers to these and other questions are not straightforward; in order to develop them, it is best to begin by examining why banks came into being and the history of the banking system.

2

Some Fundamentals

Banks used to perform essential financial services that no other institution could provide. But they also caused recurring financial instability and often abused their tremendous economic power. This chapter discusses why banks were a source of both good and evil, and it lays the groundwork for arguing in later chapters that technological and financial innovations have so altered the financial environment that little in the economics of the situation makes banking special any longer. Banks today do provide unique services, but this is primarily because of government-imposed specialization, not fundamental economic forces.

Two services traditionally made banks special. One was monetary services, which included not only providing deposit accounts allowing cash withdrawals and payments to be made by check or direct funds transfer but also executing the transfer of funds and performing the accounting that accompanied them. The other service was provision of loans to business. Each was important in its own right, but combined they gave banks a singular importance. There was a symbiotic relation between banks' monetary and loan activities. They used money deposited in accounts payable on demand as the primary means of funding loans. This practice was hazardous, as the nation discovered repeatedly in the nineteenth and early twentieth centuries, and it led to the banking collapse of the 1930s.

The basic problem, as old as banking itself, is that banks borrowed short-term and lent long-term. Their liabilities were perfectly liquid, payable on demand at par, but their loans were illiquid. Generally speaking, there was no market for used loans; they could be liquidated only as borrowers paid them off at maturity. Those loans that could be sold typically went at substantial discounts—far below par. When the public feared that banks could not meet their deposit obligations, large withdrawals occurred. If substantial enough, these withdrawals could force banks to default on their obligations because they lacked sufficient liquid reserves to cover the withdrawals.

On the surface, funding illiquid loans with liabilities that are payable on demand at par seems poor practice. But when the public had confidence in banks it worked quite well. Banks were a potent form of financial intermediary in normal times. Conversely, they could be a destructive financial intermediary when times were bad. A look at the economic forces and principles essential for evaluating banking's historical, current, and prospective roles will explain why this is so.

People discovered the usefulness of money thousands of years ago; it eliminated the need to engage in barter—the exchange of such physical commodities as wheat for clothing and other items. Farmers sold their wheat for money, which they could in turn exchange for the items they wanted to purchase. The invention of money made it far easier for people to specialize in activities they did best, allowing tremendous increases in production.

Gold and silver often served as money; coins of various denominations were struck, which further expedited trade and exchange. This money was highly useful but also bulky and subject to theft. A common practice of leaving gold or silver coins with goldsmiths and other reputable businesses therefore evolved. Those who left—deposited—their coins received a receipt or deposit slip entitling them to reclaim the amount deposited on demand. Depositing the coins increased safety, and the practice led to two important innovations. In commercial centers, it became common practice for merchants and others to instruct goldsmiths to transfer funds from one deposit account to another, taking care of necessary accounting. This eliminated the need for physical withdrawals of gold for payment and subsequent redeposit by the recipient. Such instructions facilitated transactions and became part of the payments system, evolving into the early forms of checking and accounting services banks provide today. In addition, the deposit slips themselves came to be used as money. Rather than exchanging deposit slips for coins at the goldsmith's to make payments, the public short-circuited the process by using the deposit slips alone. These pieces of paper circulated as money because they entitled the holder to claim coins on demand. And so bank notes were born.

Goldsmiths thus had become depositories, issuers of paper money, and facilitators of transactions by processing checks and shifting account balances. They provided a substantial economic benefit to the public; the safety and convenience was valuable, so valuable that people were willing to pay a fee for the services. As long as the goldsmiths left the gold coins in their vaults, the only profits available were these fees.[1]

As long as goldsmiths stayed out of the lending business, they could provide monetary services to their customers with considerable safety. In the absence of fraud or theft the goldsmiths could always meet their obligations because their liabilities never exceeded the coins in their vaults. Risks arose when these functions were combined with lending.

Banks are not, of course, simply purveyors of monetary services; they lend out their depositors' money as well. This also constituted a huge contribution to economic development. Let us consider why borrowing and lending occur and what banks' historical role in lending has been.

There are businesses and households that do not have sufficient current income or wealth to purchase items they want, though they expect to earn income in the future to cover the expenditures. For example, a business may want to buy a new machine that will enhance its profitability or a family may want to purchase a home. For want of a better term, these businesses and households are called "deficit units." At the same time, other businesses and households have income and wealth in excess of their current needs. They are "surplus units." There is a basis for a deal between these haves and the have-nots: the deficit units need to induce surplus units to make funds available but must keep the inducements small enough so that it remains worthwhile to use the funds.

The inducements involve offering surplus units the opportunity to share in the deficit units' future profits or income. The specific forms of sharing differ, but all involve selling to surplus units claims to a portion of the deficit units' future profits or income. The deal is attractive to surplus units only if they expect to receive sufficiently more than they

1. The current money order business is an example of how fees are paid for payments services.

put into the deal to compensate them for the loss of liquidity and risk that is entailed. In some cases a deal is possible, but in others surplus units require greater compensation than deficit units can afford to pay.

One arrangement is for a deficit unit to offer ownership shares to surplus units. For example, a business wanting to buy new machinery but lacking the resources to do so can sell ownership interests, allowing investors to share in the profits that are realized from the enterprise. Ownership shares have various forms ranging from partnerships to shares traded on stock exchanges. But they all have the common characteristic of entitling their holders to a claim on profits that the issuing firm might earn. These shares have been, and continue to be, an important means by which financial resources are shifted from surplus to deficit units. There are substantial difficulties, however, that limit their attractiveness to both parties.

Consider the situation of an individual who is in a surplus position and is contemplating the purchase of an ownership share in a business. The individual would be entitled to a share of the firm's profits but would also be subject to sharing in losses, which could be substantial.[2] In order to assess the attractiveness of taking an ownership interest, the individual with a surplus requires a great deal of information and must engage in substantial guesswork about how profitable the firm will be. What are the prospects for the firm's industry, and what is the role of the particular firm in it? How reputable is current management? What say, if any, does the investor have in the operation of the firm? How candid is the firm in representing its true position? And so on. It is time-consuming, costly, and difficult for a potential investor to make an informed judgment. Considerable expertise is required in assessing the potential returns and risks, and even the best-informed investor can be sadly surprised by the turn of events. Many surplus units lack both the expertise for evaluating the future prospects of a firm and the tolerance for risk required to take an ownership interest.

Those surplus units that are attracted to ownership shares often will only purchase stock issued by major businesses. The prospects for these firms are discussed widely in the financial press and by various experts, making it easier for an investor to make an informed judgment. This makes it difficult and frequently impossible for smaller businesses, for which information is often hard to obtain and evaluate, to obtain funds through offering ownership shares.

2. With limited liability, as in a corporation or limited partnership, the loss cannot exceed the amount invested in the project by the surplus unit.

Smaller businesses are also hampered in finding purchasers of their ownership shares by the illiquidity of the investment. Surplus units are locked into their ownership shares unless and until they can arrange sale to others. Sales can be effected quickly and at relatively low cost for the shares of large firms traded on major stock exchanges. But for surplus units holding the stock of smaller companies not traded on the exchanges or holding partnership interests, sales can be time-consuming and costly. Because surplus units might not be able to withdraw quickly from ownership arrangements with small firms should the funds be needed for another use, these firms have difficulty finding buyers for shares. Finally, deficit units may shy away from selling ownership interests because they do not like the prospect of sharing large gains with outsiders or want to be subjected to their pressures.

Some of the problems deficit units encounter in attracting funds from surplus units can be reduced by offering debt contracts (loans) rather than ownership shares. Less information is required for surplus units to make decisions, and the risk and liquidity characteristics of a loan may be more attractive than for an ownership share.

With a conventional debt contract, a surplus unit advances funds to a deficit unit in return for a promise to receive periodic payments of interest and repayment of the amount advanced (the principal) at a specific maturity date. A loan differs substantially from a share. Whereas the income earned on an ownership share fluctuates with the profitability of the enterprise, the income on a loan is constant and is, therefore, largely independent of the fortunes or misfortunes of the borrower.[3] As long as the borrower earns enough to make the interest payments and return the amount borrowed at maturity, a lender does not have to be concerned about how profitable the enterprise is.

Loans greatly reduce assessment problems for surplus units. For the lender, it is necessary only to assess the chances that the borrower will be unable to make the payments of interest and principal. That is, the problem is reduced to determining the probability of default. Though hardly a trivial exercise, this is simpler than trying to judge the probabilities of varying degrees of profitability or loss necessary when contemplating an ownership share.

Debt contracts allow lenders to limit even further the amount of risk they face. By requiring that a loan be secured by specific assets, the lender can take over this collateral in the event of default. For example,

3. This is true for loans with a fixed interest rate. Loans with variable interest rates generate a variable income, but even in this case the income is largely independent of the fortunes or misfortunes of the borrower.

the lender can seize machines that secure a loan to finance them. The more valuable the borrower's assets, the lower the lender's risk. In addition, even in the absence of specific collateral, the greater the borrower's initial net worth (equity position), the larger is the safety margin for the lender should the borrower suffer losses. Suppose, for example, that a firm has sufficient resources to finance half of the purchase price of a new machine and borrows the remaining 50 percent. Further suppose that the project is not successful. Rather than earning enough to pay interest and principal on the loan plus a profit to the borrower, a loss is sustained. The borrower is still obligated to pay interest and principal on the loan. As long as the loss does not exceed the 50 percent put up by the borrower, the lender will be paid. The borrower may be wiped out, but the lender is protected. Clearly, other things being equal, the larger the borrower's stake in the project, the lower the risk to the lender and the greater the risk to the borrower.

Lenders' insistence that borrowers have substantial stakes (equity positions) in the projects being financed has the direct benefit of providing a protective pad against possible losses sustained by borrowers, and it has a substantial indirect benefit as well. Borrowers have more information about the riskiness of projects than do lenders, who are limited to general knowledge about the kind of activity that is being financed, the prospects of the industry in question, and broad economic trends. But evaluating the risk of a loan also requires information about the specific project, and this information can only be provided by borrowers, who may be less than candid about a project's prospects. With a debt contract, the lender does not share in the benefits from unusual profits but does share in the costs of unusual losses (if large losses occur, the borrower is out only his stake in the project; the rest is absorbed by the lender), an asymmetry that gives the borrower incentive to underplay the risks when obtaining a loan and to take on more risk once a loan is obtained. These perverse incentives are blunted by requiring the borrower to have a substantial stake in the project.[4] Equity positions by borrowers are thus crucial elements in obtaining funds. This is true not only for businesses but for households who obtain loans for houses, cars, and other consumer durables as well.

Before turning to the role of banks as lenders it is useful to explain why businesses and households can also gain by obtaining a loan rather

---

4. The perverse incentives created by small equity positions help explain why many banks and even more S&Ls with small equity positions were willing to take on so much risk. Their stockholders gained in the event of large profits whereas the government insurance programs absorbed most of the large losses.

than selling equity shares. Borrowers benefit from not having to share any unusual gains with lenders. Interest and principal are fixed claims; after paying them, the borrower keeps any earnings that remain. Furthermore, borrowers do not have to share management decisions as much as they would with owners, and as long as defaults do not occur they are not held accountable for earnings by lenders. Lenders care only that earnings are sufficient to cover their fixed claims for interest and principal. Shareholders have a much greater interest in how well the enterprise does.

Although individual surplus units may be more willing to lend funds to businesses and households than to take on ownership interests in their affairs, the impediments to direct contact between deficit and surplus units remain great.[5] Borrowers still have to find individual lenders willing to advance funds, and though the prospect of earning interest might be a powerful inducement to potential lenders, the impediments are obvious. The information requirements are less for lending than for ownership interests, but surplus units frequently have no knowledge of the financial condition of borrowers except perhaps of the largest businesses, and often lack the talent and inclination to find out. It is difficult for individual lenders to assess the risks, to establish and enforce the appropriate equity positions for borrowers, and to provide the monitoring necessary to keep borrowers from engaging in risky projects once loans are granted.

In addition, the illiquidity of loans makes them unattractive to many surplus units. As with ownership shares, surplus units can withdraw from loans by selling them to others. Bonds issued by major corporations enjoy an active market, so such sales can and do occur, but the debts of lesser knowns are not actively traded, making them illiquid. Unlike ownership shares, debt contracts are naturally terminated at maturity. Short-term loans afford some protection against unforeseen needs for cash, but the protection is complete only if debts are payable, and paid, on the lender's demand. Most borrowers are not in a position to repay their loans on demand. They want a fixed maturity, which, in the absence of markets for used loans, makes their loans illiquid. And few potential lenders are willing to commit a sizable amount of their wealth to a single borrower; there is too much risk. A would-be borrower might be able to convince a surplus unit to provide some funds,

5. Advances in technology and information in recent years have greatly reduced these impediments, leading to more frequent direct contact between deficit and surplus units. This has, among other things, lessened the role of banks.

but often not enough to finance the entire desired expenditure. It would then be necessary to repeat the loan-negotiation process several times to find enough lenders to advance the needed funds, a time-consuming and costly venture.

Before the development of banking, lending was largely restricted to families, friends, and a relatively few wealthy individuals. Borrowing was necessarily of limited magnitude, which stifled economic development, while many worthwhile and productive activities went begging because the wealth that others had accumulated could not be mobilized. But when banks combined their monetary functions with lending, they created an effective method of using debt contracts to bridge the gap between surplus and deficit units, freeing a vast amount of wealth for productive uses.

To understand how banks began lending, consider again the goldsmiths who accepted deposits of gold coins. They noticed that withdrawals by one customer tended to be offset by deposits from another, leaving the amount of gold in the vaults relatively constant. Since the gold in storage far exceeded the amount needed to meet net withdrawals (deposits less withdrawals) on any given day, it did not take long for enterprising goldsmiths to realize that it was possible to earn interest income by lending most of the gold and still have enough left on reserve in their vaults to meet withdrawals. This, in its most basic form, is what today's fractional-reserve banks do, accepting deposits payable on demand, setting aside a small fraction of these liabilities as reserves, and using the remainder to fund loans. By combining the monetary (depository and payments) and loan functions, banks became a potent financial intermediary channeling funds from surplus to deficit units.

We have already seen the attraction of banks as purveyors of monetary services; their contribution on the loan side was no less important. By pooling depositors' funds for lending, banks were able to cut through many of the problems that had inhibited extensions of credit. Most important, they had large sums of money available for lending, and this gave them sufficient scale to justify retaining staffs with substantial knowledge of a number of industries and specific borrowers. Banks could effectively evaluate applicants' prospects for success, including adequacy of equity positions, and could keep informed by establishing long-standing relationships with their borrowers. In addition, banks' expertise allowed them to monitor borrowers after loans were granted, providing protection against undue risk taking. In short, banks became efficient processors and evaluators of information on the creditworthiness of deficit units.

Banks could also achieve other tremendous economies of scale. Before the entry of banks, each surplus unit had to engage in its own credit analysis, and in attempting to raise enough money, a borrower typically had to deal with many individuals, trying to tailor each loan to the needs of each lender. For example, if one hundred individual loans were required to fund a project, credit analyses were done one hundred times and the borrower had to negotiate one hundred loans. With a bank able to provide the entire financing, the credit analysis had to be done only once (and usually better) and only one loan needed to be negotiated. This provided huge savings to borrowers. Furthermore, bank resources were usually large relative to the needs of individual borrowers, which allowed banks to diversify by granting many different loans. Diversification ensured that the fortunes of any one borrower had relatively little effect on the performance of a bank's loans in the aggregate. In addition, because the level of deposit accounts at a bank usually remained relatively constant, with deposits roughly balancing withdrawals, the bank could employ its stable source of funding to grant the relatively long-term loans desired by borrowers.

The economies of scale achieved by banks drastically reduced the costs and risks of lending, leading to a substantial increase in the availability of credit. Banks had much to offer borrowers, and lending was profitable. But banks' ability to earn profits was limited by the amount of funds that surplus units were willing to leave with them. They therefore had incentive to offer more attractive monetary services in order to attract more deposits. The quest for greater deposits induced them to offer better payment services, to lower or eliminate service charges, to offer more convenient locations, and to pay interest on account balances. This led to extensive use of bank accounts by the public; indeed, bank competition for deposits meant that much of the gain from lending was passed on to depositors in the form of improved monetary services and interest payments on account balances.

During normal times, banks could lend a great deal. Their deposit liabilities tended to fluctuate relatively little and in a predictable manner even though individual customers might make large deposits or withdrawals. Offsetting deposit inflows and outflows gave banks sufficient stability of their demand obligations to allow them to hold only a small fraction as reserves, using the remainder to grant loans. A relatively small amount of reserves supported a large amount of deposit liabilities and loans. This was the magic of fractional-reserve banking. A bank could offer highly liquid liabilities (deposit accounts) to the public and use most of the funds to support illiquid loans whose maturity exceeded the maturity of deposits by a substantial margin. Banks, in effect, converted the highly liquid assets of depositors into illiquid assets (loans). This is what made banks such a potent financial inter-mediary. They met the liquidity needs of surplus units, mobilizing the funds to serve the borrowing requirements of deficit units. As long as the public retained faith in banks, funding relatively long-term, illiquid loans with short-term, liquid liabilities was not such a poor practice after all.

By lending to banks—their deposit accounts were loans—rather than to ultimate borrowers, surplus units did not have to sacrifice liqui-dity. What about the risk that a bank would default on its debt (deposit liabilities)? Here banks offered their lender-depositors a significant ad-vantage. Even in the absence of deposit insurance, bank deposit lia-bilities were usually much less risky than direct loans by surplus units to ultimate borrowers. This may seem strange since depositors' money was used by banks to make the very loans that surplus units usually found too risky to grant, but banks could lend at substantially lower risk because of their economies in evaluating, monitoring, and diversifying loans. Furthermore, the equity positions put up by banks' owners pro-vided protective cushions, reducing the chance that loan losses would cause banks to default on their obligations to depositors.[6] Without deposit insurance, however, the accounts (debt contracts) issued to depositors were not free of default risk. Although lending to a bank was usually far less risky and cumbersome than lending directly to deficit units, depositors still needed to evaluate and monitor the bank to which they lent. In spite of the difficulties that this entailed, the liquidity and relatively low risk of bank accounts made them highly attractive to the public.

When everything was operating smoothly, banks did an effective job of mobilizing funds by providing surplus units with monetary services while putting their account balances to work financing the develop-ment of new businesses and the growth of existing ones. This is why banks have been such an important part of the nation's financial system; they were a marvelously effective financial intermediary.

What about the problems associated with banking? Ironically, uncon-trolled banking could devastate the national welfare precisely because of its effectiveness in providing financial intermediary services. Banks' monetary and loan services were so attractive that the public came to

6. Today depositors are protected by insurance, putting the insurance fund at risk. Attempts to limit this risk explain why the bank regulators have imposed bank capital requirements.

use them extensively and to depend upon them. This in turn made depositors and borrowers highly dependent on bank safety. Their very efficiency and convenience gave banks such economic importance that they could make or break individuals, industries, and potentially even governments. Rather than banks consistently serving society's needs, society suffered the consequences of episodes of banking instability. The banking tail could wag the public dog.

The potential for problems emanated both from banking's monetary and lending activities. On the monetary side, the public came to use bank deposits payable on demand as money, with payments made initially with bank notes and later by check and wire transfer. The convenience of bank money was so great that it became the primary form in which the public held and used money.[7] Bank money worked just fine as long as banks could make good on their liabilities. People were willing to use checking accounts and to accept checks written against them in payment for services and products as long as they believed that banks could meet their obligations. But before the creation of deposit insurance, holders of bank accounts and recipients of bank notes or checks were left with worthless pieces of paper when banks failed. Furthermore, the failure of an individual bank or a few banks, or some other unfavorable event such as a sharp rise in business bankruptcies or collapse of stock or bond markets, could trigger a loss of confidence in banking, producing massive withdrawals that could lead to additional failures as otherwise solvent banks attempted to liquidate loans to meet these bank runs.

Just as the public came to depend upon banks for monetary services, borrowers also developed a dependency on banks that made them vulnerable to reductions in the availability of credit. During good times banks were a welcome source of credit, but the collapse of a bank not only ruined its depositors; it could also wipe out borrowers who still had to repay their loans and lacked alternative sources of credit. When depositors lost faith in banks generally and staged runs, many banks failed, causing a large reduction in the overall supply of bank credit. In addition, even banks that survived, trying to deal with actual or prospective runs, called in what loans they could and refused to extend additional credit in efforts to add to their reserves of liquid assets. The supply of credit could collapse and with it the economy.

Fractional-reserve banking was plagued by episodes of instability

7. Today approximately 70 percent of all money held by Americans is in the form of checking accounts; the remaining 30 percent is coins and currency. But over 98 percent of the value of transactions each year uses bank money.

during which there were widespread bank failures, collapses in the amount of bank deposits and credit, and serious disruption of services. This terrible defect surfaced relatively infrequently,[8] but its devastating effects haunted fractional-reserve banking in the United States from the beginning. The New Deal reforms following the catastrophic collapse of the banking system in the early 1930s seemed to eliminate banking's instability, but there have been disturbing signs in recent years that the cure was not permanent. It is critical, then, to identify the sources of this instability.

Once banks ceased to be simple depositories and began to extend credit, the nature of their deposit liabilities changed fundamentally. As long as banks' deposit liabilities were simply claim checks against money in their vaults, they could reliably promise to meet withdrawals on demand. When a depositor made a withdrawal, the banker simply went into the vault and got the money that was deposited. This is little different from exchanging a claim check for a coat or briefcase at a restaurant. Absent theft or fraud, the money, coat, or briefcase can be produced. When banks got into the lending business, however, the claim checks turned into private debt instruments backed by the loans and other assets banks held. Although banks continued to promise to pay at par on demand, it was no longer a sure thing that they could make good on their obligations, which were no longer fully backed by money in the vault. As financial intermediaries, banks were borrowing from one element of the public and lending to another. The public still tended to view their deposits as claim checks when in fact they had become debt contracts. Although banks could achieve great economies in risk pooling and in providing liquidity, they could not always fulfill their promise either to repay their debts in full (at par) or to repay them on demand.

The inability of banks to fulfill their promise to repay deposit obligations at par stemmed from the same sources as default on any debt contract: losses caused by bad luck, misjudgment and mismanagement, or fraud, coupled with insufficient equity to pay off creditors. When a bank's losses from any source exceeded its initial equity, the bank was insolvent; its liabilities were greater than its assets. Even when all good loans were repaid and other assets converted into cash, not enough remained to pay off depositors in full. As with any debt contract, the chances of a bank defaulting on its obligations were smaller if it possessed relatively larger equity before experiencing misfortune.

8. There were at least fourteen general banking panics from 1814 through 1933.

In the absence of deposit insurance, deposit balances were private debt contracts with all attendant risk. It behooved depositors to monitor their banks' activities to determine the extent of equity protection relative to the risks being taken, and to take their business elsewhere if their banks appeared to be too risky. This was no easy assignment. It was difficult to determine the riskiness of a bank's loan portfolio, to assess the quality of its management or its vulnerability to fraud. Past performance was not always a reliable guide for the future; even if a bank had been safe in the past there was no guarantee that it would continue to be. The problems were compounded by the lack of reporting requirements for banks that could lead to disclosure of pertinent information. With limited information, large and small depositors alike were flying in the dark. Only large depositors typically had the sophistication to evaluate what little information was available. It fell mainly on them to monitor and control bank risk taking. To the extent that they were successful, small depositors also benefited.

In principle, one protection depositors enjoyed against the chance that a bank's equity was insufficient to absorb losses was the ability to withdraw funds at the first sign that their bank might be in trouble. This was one of the attractions of a debt instrument payable on demand: a depositor would have time to get out before the bank failed. Unfortunately, this "protection" could cause a weakened but solvent bank to fail, and it made the banking system susceptible to collapse. When depositors lost faith in the ability of their bank to honor its obligations, they rushed to take the money out of their accounts. This could entail either shifting funds to banks that were viewed as sound or withdrawing currency or specie (gold and silver coins). Everyone had incentive to get to the bank first while it could still honor withdrawals. When customers feared that their money was not safe, it was rational for them to stage a run.

A single solvent bank or even a few solvent banks could withstand a run if they could borrow quickly enough from other banks. Such borrowing was often possible because lending banks often received the funds that had been withdrawn from the bank experiencing a run and because they knew that the borrowing bank was solvent and could repay its loans. If banks experiencing runs could obtain credit quickly, they could honor withdrawals. Customers would then redeposit the funds once they were convinced that the bank was viable.

If a bank was not known by other banks, however, or if it was in a weakened condition with relatively little equity, a run could cause it to fail because it could not borrow from other banks. After using up its liquid reserves, the bank would try to meet deposit withdrawals by refusing to renew maturing loans, instead demanding repayment of principal. This largely self-defeating process created great stress on the borrowers, who had expected their loans to be renewed. Many could not repay their loans and so defaulted. The bank would then seize any assets the hapless borrowers possessed, selling them for whatever the market would bear. When the smoke had cleared, the bank could often obtain only a small fraction of the value of the loan, which in and of itself could drive the bank into insolvency as the value of its assets shrank below its liabilities. Efforts to sell loans that had not yet matured took another step toward insolvency. In granting the loans, the bank possessed information about the creditworthiness of borrowers that was difficult to communicate quickly to potential purchasers, who feared that the bank would try to unload its worst loans. Those loans that could be sold quickly would fetch only a few cents on the dollar.

When the public lost faith in banks generally, funds were not shifted from questionable banks to stronger ones. Rather, people attempted to abandon bank accounts altogether by making withdrawals of currency and specie. Banks could not borrow from one another to meet the withdrawals because each was trying to deal with its own run. With many customers demanding payment at the same time, it was impossible to make good on the promise to allow withdrawals on demand. Because reserves were only a fraction of deposit liabilities, customer withdrawals could not be honored. Banks had to renege on their promise to pay on demand at par.

Coping with large losses of deposits and depletion of reserves by refusing to renew maturing loans and by selling outstanding loans was even less successful during a general banking panic than when runs were restricted to only a few weak banks. With many banks trying to sell existing loans at the same time, what sales as did occur were at distressed prices. Rapid reduction in loans during a general panic was a sure path to insolvency. The banking system as a whole simply could not quickly transform its illiquid loans into liquid assets; all it had available for quick payout were its relatively small reserves of liquid assets.

Faced with the prospect of insolvency because of trying to reduce loans quickly, banks' next measure was to refuse to provide convertibility of deposits into currency and specie. Banks continued to allow withdrawals on demand if they represented checks written to third parties for redeposit in other banks. This kept the deposit balances and reserves within the banking system and provided scope for interbank lending. But with inconvertible accounts, the public stood to lose a lot if and when some banks failed. This led to first notes and then checks that were accepted only at a discount, where the size of the discount mirrored the probability that the bank would fail in the relatively near future.

Depositors were clearly hurt by the suspension of convertibility, and borrowers were also injured because new credit was not available. Still, the alternative was worse. Better to have most banks kept afloat by suspending convertibility in the hope that the panic would subside and things return to normal than to suffer widespread bank insolvencies. Sometimes this worked and sometimes it did not.

In the absence of government intervention, a fractional-reserve banking system can be unstable. Although banks can (and many did) take steps to maintain depositor confidence by holding liquid reserves, arranging for interbank loans, and maintaining substantial capital, they simply cannot hold enough reserves of liquid assets to allow them to pay off all their depositors at once, at par, while still lending. A fractional-reserve system is the magic of banking, but it can become evil magic in a purely private system.

Monetary and credit stability requires government policies to avert widespread bank runs. But efficacious government intervention must also permit fundamental economic forces room to determine the flow of resources from surplus to deficit units and to control bank risk. Government programs put in place during the 1930s providing for deposit insurance and a strong central bank eliminated bank runs, but the approach to bank regulation developed at that time, though effective for many years, is now out of touch with these fundamental economic forces and is adding to the problems of banking.

3

The Evolution of Banking

in the United States

Banking developed differently from such industries as automobile manufacturing or health services. In other industries, technological change, competition, and consumer tastes are paramount. These concepts are, of course, meaningful in banking, but until recently they were of secondary importance. The history of banking is largely a chronicle of struggles between bankers attempting to maximize profits and government seeking to limit the power and instability of banks. Intertwined have been conflicts between the federal government and the states over who should control banks. It is difficult to overemphasize these struggles. They have molded the current structure of banking and the way it is regulated; they have colored the way that the public views banks; and they set the stage for banking's current problems.

The nation began its banking history in 1782 with the Bank of North America, founded in Philadelphia; a decade later fourteen banks were operating in twelve cities. These early banks were geared to commercial customers, providing notes and depository services while granting short-term loans to finance sales of commodities. They were subject to nominal supervision by the states in which they were chartered.

The federal government first entered the banking picture in 1791 by establishing the Bank of the United States at the urging of Secretary of the Treasury Alexander Hamilton, who sought a safe depository for federal tariff receipts and a convenient vehicle for making federal expenditures on "public improvements." The bank reflected Hamilton's desire to establish a strong federal presence in the nation's banking affairs, designed along the lines of institutions operating in European countries. The federally chartered institution had its head office in Philadelphia and branches in other cities in several states. The bank was a joint venture between the federal government and private individuals, and as such was both a profit-oriented firm and a government institution involved in efforts to improve the nation's monetary and banking systems. It accepted deposits from, and granted loans to, the federal government and dealt with private customers in competition with state-chartered banks. Both the federal bank and state-chartered banks accepted deposits of specie or bank notes and issued their own notes, redeemable for specie, to depositors and borrowers.

The bank's size and geographic reach allowed it to operate much as a central bank, using the amount of credit it extended to regulate the total quantity of credit in the economy. Further, customers often deposited notes issued by state-chartered banks with the federal bank, and the sizable holdings of these notes allowed the bank to flex its financial muscle against state institutions. If a state-chartered bank was deemed to be extending too much credit, the federal bank would demand redemption of that bank's notes for specie. In meeting the redemption, the state-chartered bank suffered a decline in its reserves and was forced to reduce its credit activities. The bank engaged in these regulatory activities at the same time that it operated in competition with state-chartered institutions.

In spite of the presence of the Bank of the United States, state-chartered banking grew over the years and by 1811 numbered eighty-eight institutions. The first bank failure occurred in 1809, when fraud brought down the Farmers Exchange Bank of Glocester, Rhode Island. But banking in general contributed to economic growth over these years. In spite of its stabilizing influence, the federal bank encountered growing opposition. Thomas Jefferson had opposed the venture from the outset, and proponents of states' rights, representatives of state-chartered banks, and state governments became increasingly hostile. Similarly, economic groups involved in agricultural expansion, who wanted greater availability of credit than the federal bank tolerated, were against it. There were complaints that the federal bank was a power unto itself, used more to line the pockets of its stockholders than to enhance growth of the economy, and in 1811 Congress refused to renew its charter.

It did not take long for state-chartered banks to develop problems. They increased note issuance dramatically during the War of 1812, at the same time that specie was flowing overseas. The fraction of notes backed by specie declined correspondingly. Risky lending and instances of fraud caused several banks to fail. The public lost faith and began to convert its holdings of notes into gold and silver. Liquidity problems developed as many banks were unable to redeem their notes for specie. These notes circulated at a discount and in some cases became worthless, inflicting great damage on their holders. Discounts on bank notes caused chaos in the nation's monetary system. The problems became particularly acute in 1814, when, following British raids, general panic set in and banks in the District of Columbia, Baltimore, New York, and Philadelphia suspended convertibility of their notes. Widespread bank failures occurred, injuring not only note holders but also those who depended upon banks as a source of credit.

The U.S. Treasury also fell victim to the chaotic banking situation, trying to finance a war with no federal bank and facing varying discounts on state-chartered banks' notes. In spite of these problems, President James Madison vetoed legislation in 1815 to reestablish a federal bank. But in 1816 he acquiesced, and the federal government again entered the picture by establishing the second Bank of the United States, which as before had headquarters in Philadelphia with branches in several states. The bank received a twenty-year charter, and, as in the case of its predecessor, ownership was divided between the federal government and private citizens, although state governments were also allocated stock.

The year 1816 also marked the birth of thrift institutions in the United States. Conventional banks provided few services for ordinary working people in the best of times, and the turbulent wartime situation had made matters worse. To fill the void in financial services, groups of philanthropically minded wealthy people in Philadelphia, New York, and Boston established, and served as trustees of, savings banks that were mutually owned by their "working-class" depositors. These mutual savings banks used the funds deposited to purchase stocks, bonds, and other assets, passing the net earnings on to their depositor-owners. An early form of the thrifts we know today, these savings banks proved immensely popular. But they were far removed from the affairs of the Bank of the United States.

Saddled initially with poor management, beset with renewed opposition from local banks and states' rights politicians, and struggling with the effects of a severe business depression, the second Bank of the United States got off to a slow start. In 1819, however, strong management was put in place under Nicholas Biddle, and the constitutionality of the federal bank was confirmed by the Supreme Court in *McCulloch v. Maryland*. The nation's currency improved markedly, and there was a strong business expansion. The Bank of the United States undertook to control the proliferation of bank notes by aggressively presenting them for redemption in cases where it believed the issues to be unsound.

Like its predecessor, the second bank's size, interstate reach, and dealings with the U.S. Treasury gave its private managers and owners immense economic power that ultimately doomed it politically. By limiting the growth of credit, the bank became increasingly unpopular with those involved in western expansion and with other proponents of easy money, who viewed the bank's actions as arbitrary and self-serving. Even though economic activity was expanding, prices were falling during the 1820s. Deflation increased the burden on debtors, leading them to clamor for lower interest rates. A rising chorus of critics claimed that the bank was the captive of special interests who benefited from high interest rates, restrictive credit, and deflation.

Criticisms were aided by banking interests in New York City seeking to undermine the federal bank. New York had surpassed Philadelphia as a commercial center, and the U.S. Treasury obtained more customs receipts from New York, yet the nation's banking center was Chestnut Street in Philadelphia rather than Wall Street in New York. Banking interests in New York worked strenuously to change the situation. They encouraged criticism of the federal bank by agrarian interests and were aided by President Andrew Jackson's influential adviser, Martin Van Buren, who was an effective spokesman for states' rights and New York interests. Jackson's belief in states' rights, his concern for agrarian issues, and his distrust of banks in general and the economically and politically powerful Bank of the United States in particular had predisposed him to oppose the bank in any case. In 1832, Jackson vetoed legislation to give the second Bank of the United States a new charter and, in anticipation of the bank's demise in 1836, ordered the U.S. Treasury to shift its business from the federal bank to state-chartered institutions. The financial center of the United States shifted to Wall Street.

In 1836, the year the second Bank of the United States disappeared, cooperative building and loan associations, through which members pooled their savings and lent to each other to finance home purchases, first got started. Members made monthly deposits toward acquisition of ownership shares in their association, entitling them to obtain loans. As these institutions grew they lost their cooperative character; they evolved into savings and loans, which along with mutual savings banks became the nation's major thrift institutions.

Following the expiration of the second Bank of the United States, and just two months after Van Buren's inauguration as president in 1837, the nation experienced a financial panic and banking collapse with widespread currency suspension. Recovery from the business decline that followed was slow, and the economy experienced price deflation. Economic growth accelerated after 1845, with heavy investment in railroads and western expansion, and prices rose. The number of banks increased and note issuance accelerated; suspensions were frequent, particularly in the West. In the nation as a whole, notes were issued by some sixteen hundred banks. Many of the new banks were sound, but all too many were simply money machines operated by larcenous owners. "Wildcat" banking was a common ruse: notes were issued by "banks" with no known address whose owners would retreat to the woods with the wildcats when note holders tried to locate them for redemption. The situation was so chaotic that the public had to consult periodicals called "bank note reporters and counterfeit detectors" to guard against worthless notes and find values of notes not locally known.

The federal government did not repeat history by establishing a third Bank of the United States. Instead, it gave up on banks altogether by establishing the Independent Treasury System in 1846. The U.S. Treasury had to hold all its funds in its own vaults in gold and silver, and all payments to and from the Treasury were in coin only. The Treasury thus bypassed banks, leaving the states and the public to cope as best they could with the banking situation.

State governments were not idle, however, and in many cases their efforts prevented the situation from becoming even worse. In 1838, New York and then other states established "free banking." This replaced the system under which charters were granted by state legislatures (which encouraged graft but still left banks unregulated) with a better one. Under free banking, any bank meeting certain criteria concerning the amount of capital put up by the organizers and the availability of liquid reserves was free to receive a charter.

The move to free banking was a step in the right direction, but banking remained in a disorderly condition. Bank credit fluctuated widely, failures were common, and bank notes were often traded at discount as banks refused convertibility. Instead of a single national currency, there were as many kinds of money in the United States as there were discounts on banks' notes.

Many states intensified the battle to control the activities of their banks, with some success. In 1842, for example, Louisiana passed the first law to require minimum reserves against deposit accounts. Before that time, reserves had been imposed only against notes. Several other states set up state banks as mini-versions of the first and second Banks of the United States, somewhat reducing the instability of the banking system. But there was not enough discipline to go around. Problems were most severe in the West, particularly in Michigan, but Indiana, Illinois, and even New York were not immune. Some areas gave up on banking entirely. For example, in 1852 there were no incorporated banks in Arkansas, California, Florida, Illinois, Iowa, Texas, or Wisconsin. There were also none in the territories of Minnesota and Oregon, or even in the District of Columbia.

Following a panic and banking collapse in 1857, the prospect of civil war further eroded the public's already weakened faith in banks, leading again to widespread inconvertibility of bank notes. The situation was made worse when, at the start of war, the federal government financed its large military expenditures through loans, in specie, extended by state-chartered banks in the North. The worsening financial condition of the government and the shaky plight of the Union, coupled with general fears about note inconvertibility in a war situation, produced panic in 1861. Large conversions of bank notes into specie by the public drained specie from banks, forcing virtually all of them to suspend convertibility of their notes.

With the resources of the banking system drying up, the government found it difficult to borrow. The United States suspended the metallic (gold and silver) standard under which notes could be redeemed at will for specie and started to print greenbacks to pay for war expenditures. These notes were not redeemable for specie, but by declaring them to be legal tender, the government induced public acceptance.

In this setting, Congress in 1863 started the transition to a purely federal currency. The National Currency Act, subsequently retitled the National Bank Act, established within the U.S. Treasury the Office of the Comptroller of the Currency to charter national banks that were authorized to issue national bank notes. National bank notes were not legal tender, but if a national bank were to fail, the U.S. Treasury would convert its notes into greenbacks. Every national bank had to accept the notes issued by any other national bank at par, and the U.S. government, by law, accepted national bank notes for payment of taxes and purchases of securities. For all intents and purposes, national bank notes and greenbacks were the same thing. This laid the groundwork for establishing a uniform currency in the United States.

The National Bank Act also returned the federal government to banking affairs. Unlike the first and second Banks of the United States, national banks did not involve joint ownership between the federal government and private parties. National banks were, and are, privately owned institutions, but they were regulated. Following the lead of the more enlightened state banking laws, minimum capital standards and other entry criteria were set for national banks; reserve requirements were imposed against notes and deposit accounts; and the Comptroller of the Currency had authority to supervise and regulate the activities of national banks.

In 1866, the federal government attempted to force conversions of state-chartered banks to national banks. By establishing a 10 percent tax on notes issued by state-chartered banks, the federal government rendered them unprofitable, and these notes soon disappeared. Finally the nation had a uniform, federal currency composed of greenbacks and national bank notes.[1] Deprived of issuing notes by the tax, many state-chartered banks converted to national banks. In 1860 there had been 1,529 state-chartered banks; by 1868 only 247 remained. But most did not cease operations. In their place stood 1,640 national banks.

The demise of state-chartered banks proved short-lived. In the years leading up to the establishment of national banks, the use of notes had already been declining relative to the use of checking accounts as improvements in communication and transport made checks increasingly attractive. The growing acceptance of checks made banking under a state charter possible, and the generally milder regulatory standards imposed by the states made these banks attractive to their owners. Once again, by the 1880s, state banks were growing rapidly, using checking accounts in place of notes.

The rebound of state-chartered banks was remarkable. By 1910 there were more than twice as many state-chartered banks as national banks. Rather than killing off state-chartered banks with its tax on their notes, leaving only federally chartered and supervised institutions, the federal government simply accelerated the use of checking accounts. After a brief hiatus, banking supervised by the states was once again an important element in the nation's banking system.

1. In 1879 the United States returned to a metallic standard and national bank notes became redeemable for specie.

National banks, too, encouraged the public to use checking accounts rather than currency (bank notes) as a means of payment, partly because they were required to back their notes with government securities, which became scarce as the amount of government debt shrank following the Civil War. Even federally controlled banks were thus able to circumvent regulatory restrictions intended to contain expansion of their liabilities.

The inflexibility in the supply of currency built into the National Bank Act unwittingly but significantly increased the vulnerability of the banking system to financial distress, exemplified by the panics of 1893 and 1907. In those years, an increase in the number of bank failures weakened public confidence. Runs occurred when holders of deposit balances demanded payment in currency—that is, in national bank notes or in gold or silver certificates issued by the government. Several banks lacked sufficient currency and could not borrow enough to meet withdrawals. Panic ensued as further runs occurred and inconvertibility became widespread. Though suspension of convertibility allowed many banks to remain solvent and ultimately protected depositors, problems were legion while it lasted. In particular, checks were often accepted in transactions only at a discount. Thus, checking accounts were no more safe than the old bank notes they replaced. A federal presence in the bank supervisory business did result in a tightening of regulatory standards, but financial panics, suspensions, and widespread bank failures still occurred. National banks failed right along with state-chartered banks.

Responding to the latest banking crisis, Congress passed the Aldrich-Vreeland Act of 1908, allowing national banks to issue additional notes in an emergency and establishing the National Monetary Commission to recommend more fundamental reform. The commission, through hearings and studies, stimulated heated debates within the government and among private citizens over how to solve the nation's banking problems. The debates, which centered around the old issues of states' rights, large versus small banks, and financial centers versus rural areas, were finally settled with the Federal Reserve Act of 1913, which gave the United States a central bank of sorts.[2] While the Federal Reserve Act was a step in the right direction, it contained flaws that were largely a result of the political compromises that had to be made to get any central bank at all. Regional interests opposed establishing a single central bank, such as existed in other industrialized nations, and states'

2. The Federal Reserve began operations in 1914.

righters resisted a substantial federal presence in the affairs of the central bank. These groups feared that a central bank would be controlled by the interests of Wall Street or Washington, D.C. Disagreement between bankers and nonbankers about whether the central bank should be a private bank for bankers or a government-operated institution led to a compromise: it was a little of both.

The "central bank" was formed as the Federal Reserve System, which was a weak confederation of twelve separate Federal Reserve banks coordinated in a loose manner by the Federal Reserve Board in Washington. Each Federal Reserve bank received a federal charter but was owned by its member banks and functioned as a bank for banks. Each issued its own currency, called Federal Reserve notes, and reserve accounts were established at each Federal Reserve bank for the member banks in its district. Member banks were also authorized to borrow from their Federal Reserve bank. National banks were required to become member banks, but membership in the Federal Reserve System was optional for state-chartered banks.

Membership in the Federal Reserve System offered several benefits. Most important, member banks could use their Federal Reserve bank to obtain currency. A Federal Reserve bank was authorized not only to honor currency withdrawals from a member bank's reserve account but also to lend funds to member banks, allowing them to get additional reserves and currency if their own holdings ran out.[3] Currency was thus to be available to banks even during crisis periods, in theory solving the problem of currency shortage that had led to the panics of 1893 and 1907.

Being a member of the Federal Reserve System involved certain costs, however. Member banks were required to hold a fraction of their deposit liabilities as reserves in the form of funds deposited at their Federal Reserve bank. These reserve balances earned no interest, unlike the reserves held with correspondent banks, and the Federal Reserve was empowered to regulate and supervise member banks. The regulatory restrictions on member banks closely followed the provisions that had been established for national banks. In effect, state-chartered member banks became subject to the same standards as national banks.

After weighing the benefits and costs of membership, relatively few state-chartered banks elected to become members. By 1922, only about 1,600 of the nearly 22,000 state-chartered banks in the country were

3. Additional reserves could also be provided through open-market operations in which a Federal Reserve bank purchased government securities, bankers' acceptances, or similar instruments.

members. Most small state-chartered banks obtained currency, loans, and check-clearing services from large correspondent banks, which in turn were mostly Federal Reserve members. Thus, nonmember banks avoided federal regulations yet enjoyed the facilities of the Federal Reserve indirectly.

The Federal Reserve Act established a fractional-reserve system for member banks, but this in itself did little to increase the stability of the banking system. When a depositor made a withdrawal from a bank, only a fraction of the loss could be met by drawing down the bank's reserve account at its Federal Reserve bank. For example, with a reserve requirement of 10 percent, a one-hundred-dollar withdrawal from a checking account reduced required reserves by ten dollars. The remaining ninety dollars had to come from any reserves held in excess of those required, from asset sales, or from borrowing. But here the Federal Reserve provided a crucial service: if a member bank experienced difficulty in borrowing from other banks or if hasty asset sales were reducing asset prices, its Federal Reserve bank would serve as lender of last resort through its "discount window."[4] In lending to a bank, the Federal Reserve bank simply added to the bank's reserve account, giving it the resources to meet withdrawals. The bank could withdraw the borrowed reserves in the form of currency and counter any bank run.

The Federal Reserve was to provide an "elastic currency," which was intended to expand when the public made currency withdrawals and contract with deposits of currency. In principle, the elasticity of currency would allow the banking system to meet public demand during panics; the Federal Reserve would lend the needed currency to member banks. When public confidence returned, the quantity of currency would automatically decline as the public redeposited funds in banks and the banks repaid their loans at the Federal Reserve's discount window.

Unfortunately, the mechanism for providing an elastic currency was badly flawed. Congress treated Federal Reserve banks much like national banks, restricting their note issuance and requiring that their reserve account liabilities be secured by certain assets. Furthermore, Federal Reserve banks were to act like commercial banks by making only "good loans"—that is, loans that were safe in accordance with accepted banking practices. To the extent that member banks lacked appropriate collateral they could not borrow from Federal Reserve banks. These

4. Federal Reserve banks had windows like tellers' windows where banks obtained loans by discounting eligible collateral. The windows have long since disappeared, but the term "discount window" remains.

restrictions and the philosophy behind them led the Fed to operate like a private bank rather than a true central bank, with disastrous consequences.

The United States survived the trauma of World War I without a banking crisis. And though bank suspensions averaged nearly six hundred per year in the 1920s, these involved mainly small rural banks and did not trigger panic. With the Federal Reserve firmly in place, the nation appeared to have exorcised its monetary and banking instability.

But clouds were gathering over the banking industry during the 1920s. With booming securities markets, businesses turned from banks to these markets as sources of finance. Banks responded by joining the party. They lent vast sums to individuals and companies to finance the acquisition of stocks and bonds, and they became actively involved through operation of affiliated companies in the underwriting, distributing, and holding of securities. They also substantially increased lending for purchases of real estate. Thus, banks helped fuel the booms in securities and real estate markets that marked the twenties.

The party ended abruptly with the stock market crash in October 1929. Banks initially survived the crash relatively unscathed, thanks in large part to the efforts of the Federal Reserve Bank of New York, whose open-market operations and loans provided banks with needed reserves. In spite of the severity of the stock market collapse, the public retained its confidence in banks; there was no banking panic in 1929. Banking crises came instead in three waves during the early 1930s.

The first crisis occurred a year later, in October 1930. Economic conditions around the country were worsening, and a sharp rise in bank failures in agricultural states snapped public confidence; bank runs began. During 1930, there were 1,350 bank failures, and in the last two months of 1930 alone, more than 600 banks went under, including a large bank that was a member of the Federal Reserve System. In the first two months of 1931 the public began to redeposit its currency. But banks were in a weakened condition because of both runs and the worsening depression that produced large loan and securities losses. Many banks sharply curtailed their lending in an effort to build up liquid reserves in the event of subsequent runs. They did not have long to wait.

In March 1931, bank failures were on the rise again and panic set in once more. The public staged runs and banks severely curtailed their lending. International developments intensified the crisis when in May, Austria's largest private bank, the Kreditanstalt, failed. This had repercussions throughout Europe, producing further failures, particularly in Germany.

The depression and financial crisis became worldwide; faced with large losses of gold and concomitant losses of bank reserves, Great Britain abandoned the gold standard in September 1931. This led to the anticipation that the United States would soon follow, and foreigners, particularly Europeans, sold dollar assets, bought gold, and exported it from the United States. Gold exports drained reserves from the U.S. banking system, amplifying the reserve losses due to domestic currency withdrawals. Reserves in the U.S. banking system plummeted. Banks sharply curtailed lending, runs intensified, and there was a spectacular increase in bank failures. For 1931 as a whole, 2,300 banks ceased operations.

An all-too-brief pause in the economic and financial decline occurred in 1932, as Congress and the Hoover administration finally reacted to the banking collapse. But it was almost as though the nation were catching its breath before continuing the downward spiral. That January the Reconstruction Finance Corporation (RFC) was established with authority to lend to banks. Its loans helped relieve pressure on beleaguered banks. In February 1932, Congress passed the Glass-Steagall Act, which broadened the collateral for Federal Reserve notes and made it easier for member banks to borrow. A proposal to provide federal deposit insurance for bank deposits passed the House of Representatives but died in the Senate. Congress pressured the Federal Reserve to do more, obtaining a sharp increase in open-market operations and a concomitant expansion in bank reserves in April 1932. This helped avert another panic following the failure of more than forty banks in Chicago. With greater availability of reserves, banks generally got some much needed breathing room, reducing the incidence of bank failures. But the improvement was only relative to the collapses in 1930–31; more than 1,450 banks closed in 1932. Those that remained were in a seriously weakened condition.

The bottom fell out in 1933. Economic conditions worsened, bank failures accelerated, and panic set in once again. Individual states began to declare bank holidays, a euphemism for closing banks under their jurisdiction, and Congress let national banks restrict withdrawals in states enforcing bank holidays. In response to congressional criticism that RFC loans were going to banks with political influence, the agency began to publish the names of banks receiving loans. This reduced public confidence in these banks, resulting in runs and an unwillingness of other banks to borrow from the RFC. Conditions worsened, and by March 1933, about half of the forty-eight states had declared banking holidays. Gold began to flow abroad in a torrent as foreign and domestic investors speculated on a devaluation of the dollar. With gold and bank reserves plunging, the Federal Reserve suspended reserve requirements. On March 4, New York declared a bank holiday, and Illinois, Massachusetts, New Jersey, and Pennsylvania quickly followed. On the same day, the Federal Reserve closed, as did the major securities exchanges. The nation's financial system was shutting down. "The central banking system, set up primarily to render impossible the restrictions of payment by commercial banks, itself joined the commercial banks in a more widespread, complete, and economically disturbing restriction of payments than had ever been experienced in the history of the country."[5] At midnight of March 6 following his inauguration, Franklin D. Roosevelt declared a national banking holiday, closing all banks and suspending gold transactions.

The Federal Reserve System had been created to prevent a banking collapse, but here was a breakdown of historic proportions. Why was central banking so unsuccessful? With panic spreading, member banks turned to their Federal Reserve banks for assistance. Federal Reserve banks did issue additional currency, made loans, and engaged in open-market operations from time to time, but not enough funds were made available to offset the loss of reserves from customers' currency withdrawals. With deteriorating economic conditions, many bank loans looked risky, so Federal Reserve banks refused to accept them as collateral for loans to member banks. Unable to obtain sufficient credit from the Federal Reserve to meet their customers' panicked withdrawals, member banks severely restricted credit and attempted to sell existing assets at progressively declining prices. Furthermore, because member banks were experiencing massive withdrawals and loans from Federal Reserve banks were scarce, member banks could not lend to nonmember banks. Nonmembers' indirect tap on the Fed was turned off. The Federal Reserve apparently believed that its own reserves and collateral would soon be insufficient to cover additional currency issues and other emergency needs; it therefore further restricted loans to member banks. The Federal Reserve System was unwilling to stop the effects of massive currency withdrawals and apparently felt that it was unable to do so. The consequence was the total collapse of the banking system.

By any standard, the Federal Reserve System performed miserably. Not only did it fail to provide desperately needed currency and reserves, but the Federal Reserve also discouraged actions by banks that

5. Friedman and Schwartz, *Monetary History of the United States,* pp. 327–28.

could have prevented such a monumental collapse. We saw earlier that before the establishment of the Federal Reserve System, banks had developed methods of coping with runs that, though far from perfect, at least blunted their effects. By suspending convertibility and establishing mechanisms for engaging in substantial interbank borrowing and lending, at least the larger solvent banks could stay afloat. Depositors and borrowers were hurt, but massive bank failures were averted and the payments system continued to function. With the Federal Reserve's promises of the availability of loans and currency, these private initiatives had largely disappeared. Compounding the problem, the Federal Reserve, confident of its ability to confront the crisis early on, required member banks to maintain convertibility. When these banks continued to lose reserves, the Federal Reserve no longer helped them, and they had no recourse but to sell assets, intensifying the collapse. In the end, many banks had to suspend convertibility anyway.

The waves of banking panic that beset the nation from 1930 to 1933 were unprecedented in magnitude and duration. Liquidity crises hit time and time again. The numbers of banks that failed or suspended operations were staggering: over 9,600 banks went out of business during the years 1930–33, with some 4,000 closures occurring in 1933 alone. National banks, state-chartered member banks, and nonmember banks were all affected. All the efforts expended by the federal and state governments during the previous century and a half to make banks safe had failed to avert calamity. The catastrophic effects for both depositors and borrowers made the banking collapse a prime contributor to the Great Depression.

The New Deal Banking Reforms

The New Deal banking reforms contained no grand design and no revolutionary approaches, just an urgent desire of both the Roosevelt administration and Congress to regain public confidence and rid banking of its instability and worst abuses. The laws enacted during Roosevelt's first term were not only successful in achieving their objectives but also highly durable; they established the structure of banking and bank regulation that exists to this day.

The new administration's first objective was to restore public confidence as quickly as possible so that banks could be reopened. This was accomplished by the Emergency Banking Act—proposed, approved by Congress, and signed into law all on March 9, only five days after the administration took office. This act required that banks receive a license of solvency before reopening and arranged for the liquidation of insolvent institutions. It authorized the RFC to acquire preferred stock in banks—returning many to solvency—and allowed the Federal Reserve banks to issue additional currency on an emergency basis. These emergency efforts allowed the banking holiday to end by March 15. Fewer than 12,000 of the 17,000-plus banks in existence were licensed to open and do business. Of the more than 5,000 unlicensed banks, over 2,000 closed permanently and approximately 3,000 opened later.

Public trust was restored, buying the administration time to develop permanent banking and financial reform legislation over the next two years. The most important reform was the erection of a federal safety net under the banking system to ensure that it would not collapse again. This safety net, which has survived for nearly six decades, has two components: federal insurance of bank accounts and Federal Reserve policies to provide reserves and currency when needed. By establishing the safety net, the federal government directly and clearly assumed responsibility for making the banking system safe.

The first component of the safety net was both simple and direct. The Federal Deposit Insurance Corporation was created to provide federal insurance for balances in bank accounts. With insurance, depositors were guaranteed by the federal government that their accounts were safe. If an insured bank could not meet its obligations to depositors, the government would quickly provide the funds. This reform was remarkable in its simplicity and success. Deposit insurance eliminated the incentive for insured depositors to stage runs.

In spite of the banking disaster, deposit insurance was neither proposed nor supported by the Roosevelt administration, which feared the potential expense, and it was opposed by several Federal Reserve officials, the American Bankers Association, and others who favored different solutions. But there was overwhelming public support for insurance, and Congress took the initiative by inserting deposit insurance in the Banking (Glass-Steagall) Act of 1933. Deposit insurance was seen by reformers as a means of achieving banking stability while retaining the existing structure with its thousands of independent banks. Previous efforts to obtain deposit insurance had been thwarted in large part by those who favored eliminating branching restrictions to produce relatively few banks with nationwide branch networks, which would enjoy greater public confidence and could withstand runs through interbank loans and coordination with the Federal Reserve. With deposit insurance, however, depositors at small banks have no more to fear than their counterparts in large banks. This was the appeal for small banks, which could compete with large banks even though they lacked the safety. In 1933, the proponents of federal deposit insurance and small independent banks finally won.

Although deposit insurance greatly lowered the chances of bank runs, it did not reduce the risk of failure from such other sources as fraud, risky loans, or poor management. But now the risk was shifted from insured depositors to the FDIC. An unfortunate by-product of deposit insurance was that it might induce banks to take on more risk than otherwise because they did not have to fear that insured depositors would withdraw their money. All banks were safe as far as insured depositors were concerned. This equal protection of safe and unsafe banks was one of the reasons for opposition to deposit insurance. With the FDIC bearing risk and with depositors imposing less discipline on banks, more of the burden fell on the federal government to control bank risk. The FDIC was therefore also given authority for regulating and supervising all insured banks. Since national banks and Federal Reserve member banks, which were required to have insurance, were already regulated and supervised by the Comptroller of the Currency and the Federal Reserve, the FDIC's role was nominal for them. But deposit insurance was also made available to the thousands of state-chartered banks that were not member banks.[6]

Through the need to limit bank risk, the FDIC became a vehicle for imposing federal regulatory standards on state-chartered banks that were not Federal Reserve System members. Because of the never-ending battle over states' rights, federal law did not require state-chartered nonmember banks to obtain insurance.[7] But the benefits of insurance were so obvious that virtually all state-chartered non-member banks obtained it. Thus, the federal government finally succeeded in bringing almost all banks under its regulatory jurisdiction.

In drafting the FDIC Act, considerable debate took place over the extent of insurance coverage and how to finance the insurance. Congress decided to provide total insurance protection to small depositors and partial protection to large depositors, eliminating the need for small depositors to try to figure out which bank was safe and which was

6. The original FDIC Act of 1933 required insured nonmember banks eventually to become members of the Federal Reserve System. This provision was repealed in 1939.

7. To this day, the federal government does not require FDIC insurance for state-chartered nonmember banks, though most states do.

not. Because they still had at least some funds at risk, large depositors continued to have an incentive to monitor their banks' safety and to shift funds from less safe to safer banks. This private incentive in principle (but unfortunately not in practice)[8] reduced the burden on the FDIC in controlling bank safety. Initially, the FDIC insured only the first $2,500 of accounts held by each depositor at each bank.[9] That limit was quickly raised to $5,000 and has been increased over the years until it now covers the first $100,000 of accounts held by each depositor at each bank.

A simple formula assessed each insured bank a flat annual fee based on its total deposit liabilities. The fee allowed the FDIC to build up an insurance fund sufficient to pay out claims to depositors when banks failed. To the extent that the fund was adequate, deposit insurance was self-financing. As a safeguard, however, the FDIC was empowered to assess additional fees if necessary and to borrow should the insurance fund be inadequate. This second provision assured that the FDIC could always meet its insurance obligations; the federal government became the ultimate guarantor of insured deposits.

The federal safety net was secured by reforms that transformed the Federal Reserve into an effective central bank that could, and would, prevent a financial collapse from reoccurring. The formerly fragmented and regional structure of the Federal Reserve System was abandoned, and in its place was erected a federal institution that has, over time, assumed explicit responsibility for regulating the amount of money and credit in the economy. The autonomy of the twelve regional Federal Reserve banks was drastically reduced and primary decision-making power centralized with a revitalized Board of Governors in Washington. A number of crucial but technical changes were made in the Federal Reserve Act relaxing or eliminating collateral and reserve restrictions, and providing an organizational structure for the use of open-market operations—purchases and sales of government securities—to control

8. In chapter 4, I argue that the FDIC's approach to handling bank failures has in effect extended government protection to all depositors, both insured and uninsured, eliminating the incentive of "uninsured" depositors to control bank safety.

9. Under the FDIC Act of 1933, the initial $2,500 coverage was a temporary measure to be replaced in six months by graduated coverage, providing complete protection for the first $10,000, 75 percent coverage for the next $40,000, and 50 percent protection for any excess over $50,000. But graduated coverage never went into effect. After several extensions of the temporary plan, Congress in 1935 adopted flat ($5,000) coverage as permanent. Though coverage has been increased over the years, it has never involved the graduated scheme found in the original act.

bank reserves.[10] Together, these changes gave the Federal Reserve the resources and impetus to provide any currency and reserves needed and to stand as the nation's ultimate source of liquidity.

In principle, it would not be necessary to have both deposit insurance and a revitalized Fed to avert banking panics; one would be enough. The FDIC, particularly if insurance covered large accounts, would be enough to prevent bank runs from occurring. The Fed's powers were also sufficient to meet a bank run should it materialize and to prevent it from spreading. In effect, Congress wove redundancy into the safety net to make it doubly strong. Responsibility for protecting the stability of the banking system lay with two separate agencies of government. This may not have been the simplest solution, and it lacked a straightforward rationale, but it was effective.

The two elements of the safety net are not the same, however, either in operation or in effect. Deposit insurance operates automatically. If a bank fails for any reason, insured depositors are protected; the FDIC has no discretion about this. Federal Reserve policies are the product of officials' deliberations. The Federal Reserve's earlier, dismal performance made reformers skeptical of its willingness to react forcefully to any future crises. Better to have an automatic deposit insurance system to go along with the Fed's discretionary policy.

The two components of the safety net also differ in what they protect. Deposit insurance shields depositors from any source of bank failure such as fraud, risky loans, or poor management, as well as from failures caused by bank runs. The Federal Reserve, in contrast, is charged with controlling the effects of bank failures once they occur. Should depositors at solvent banks stage runs, the Fed is ready to provide the reserves, currency, and credit to keep the banking system from being affected. The Federal Reserve, in principle, is responsible for protecting the banking *system*, not for protecting individual banks or their depositors.[11]

Federal deposit insurance and an effective central bank eliminated banking panics and disastrous bank failures. After almost a century and a half, stability of the fractional-reserve banking system had been achieved.

10. Open-market operations became the responsibility of the Federal Open Market Committee, composed of the seven Federal Reserve governors in Washington and five of the twelve Federal Reserve bank presidents serving on a revolving basis.
11. Of course, the Fed has been very much in the business of protecting individual failed banks in recent years. The effects of this unfortunate practice are discussed in chapter 4.

Other important financial reforms were enacted in the 1930s. Some worked by virtually any standard, but others were at best a mixed blessing. Some bank failures had been the result of unsavory, if not fraudulent, activities. These practices involved large unsecured loans granted to bank officers or major stockholders and questionable loans granted to companies owned by them. Employees and stockholders also used bank loans to manipulate prices in market securities. Congress therefore placed severe restrictions on banks' ability to lend to members of their boards of directors, bank officers, or other employees. Although instances of insider abuse continue to this day and have contributed to some recent bank failures, Congress drastically limited the practice.

The Securities Acts outlawed the unsavory and often ruinous practices of the 1920s in which underwriters, large securities holders, and others duped the public, manipulated the prices of securities, used inside information, and engaged in practices involving egregious conflicts of interest. Through the newly formed Securities and Exchange Commission (SEC), standards were set for disclosure of pertinent information to investors concerning the financial condition and management of firms whose securities were sold to the general public. The securities exchanges were placed under federal regulation, and situations involving possible price manipulation, use of insider information, and conflicts of interest were policed.

It is important in this discussion of New Deal banking reforms to recognize what the securities laws accomplished because misunderstanding exists about restrictions on banks' securities operations imposed by the Glass-Steagall Act of 1933. Following the stockmarket crash of 1929 and the avalanche of bank failures, Congress staged hearings on the role of banks in manipulating stock and bond markets. At that time, banks held corporate stocks and bonds, underwrote corporate securities, and brokered and dealt in corporate securities. Some bankers bid up the prices of securities before selling them to the public and sold securities when they had inside information that the firm involved was in financial difficulty. In response to these revelations, the Glass-Steagall Act took banks out of the business of underwriting, dealing, and brokering in corporate securities.[12] But this reform was less

---

12. Banks were allowed to continue many other activities where equally undesirable practices were possible. For example, they could underwrite the general obligation bonds of state and local governments; they were allowed to serve as dealers for government securities and foreign exchange; and they were not forced to give up their trust activities. Apparently, abuses in these areas during the 1920s were not sufficiently noteworthy to induce Congress to prohibit them.

important than it might appear because the Securities Acts would have reformed bank behavior anyway. In recent years the Glass-Steagall Act has become a major bone of contention for banks seeking to enter new activities as securities firms have increasingly provided banking services.

Some 1930s legislation sought to limit competition among banks as a means of enhancing profitability and strengthening the banking industry. It was widely believed in Congress and elsewhere that "overbanking" and "destructive competition" caused many bank failures in the 1930s. This approach was very different from the one taken in establishing the federal safety net, which protected the banking *system,* preventing a single bank failure or other financial disturbance from building into a panic that could bring the whole financial structure crashing down. In contrast, changes in the regulatory environment directed at protecting banks from competition sought to keep individual banks sufficiently profitable that they would not fail in the first place. If no bank is allowed to fail, the banking system cannot fail, but at great cost in terms of stifled innovation, inefficiency, and all the other side effects of trying to protect an industry.

What were the measures that sought to promote profitability of individual banks through restricting competition? At the cornerstone were limitations on the formation of new banks. Congress believed that over-banking had led to many failures in the 1930s because banks had taken on increasingly risky business in a vain effort to remain profitable. By limiting the number of banks, it was argued, such excesses could be avoided. Severe restrictions on granting charters to new national banks were imposed, and new state-chartered banks found it difficult to obtain federal deposit insurance. These policies kept existing banks well protected, though restrictions on new charters have been greatly reduced in recent years. In addition, by retaining the restrictions on national banks in the McFadden Act (passed in 1928), the federal government agreed to respect state restrictions on branching: no bank was allowed to branch across state lines, and several states maintained tight limits on within-state branching.

Restrictions on branching were defended as a means of preventing small banks from being forced out of business by large ones that could establish vast branch networks. Although the branching restrictions had this effect, they often allowed existing banks to monopolize markets. Adhering to the branching restrictions of the states to protect small banks is the equivalent of banning new Safeway stores on the ground that they would threaten mom and pop groceries or arguing that there would be far more American car manufacturers today if General Motors, Ford, and Chrysler could sell only within their home states. This is no doubt true, but at what cost? Branching restrictions have been reduced recently by several states, and will probably disappear in the not too distant future.

The federal government also tried to aid bank profitability by imposing ceilings on the interest rates that banks could pay for deposits. It was argued that competition among banks had pushed interest rates on deposit accounts to unreasonable heights, forcing banks to grant risky loans at high interest rates in order to earn profits. When loans fell into default in the early 1930s, many banks failed. Congress concluded that if ceilings were imposed on the interest rates banks paid for their liabilities, they would not acquire highly risky assets and would therefore be less likely to fail. Although there was virtually no evidence to support this assertion at the time (careful studies since have also found no evidence of such destructive competition), Congress imposed the ceilings. Interest payments on demand deposit accounts—accounts that Congress tried to make a commercial bank monopoly—were flatly prohibited; for other accounts, the federal regulators were authorized to set ceilings. Because deposits are the largest element of cost for a bank, it appeared that limiting or prohibiting the interest rates paid would be a tremendous boon to profitability. For a time it did augment bank profits, but as we shall see, this did not prove true in the long run.

Although failures and runs had been much less of a problem for thrift institutions than for banks, deposit insurance was provided for thrifts as well. Insurance was made available for mutual savings banks through the FDIC,[13] and accounts at savings and loan associations (S&Ls) were insured by the Federal Savings and Loan Insurance Corporation. The special treatment of S&L accounts was part of a program to give these institutions their own federal regulatory apparatus consistent with their newly appointed role as vehicles for improving housing finance. Federal charters were made available for S&Ls, and the Federal Home Loan Bank System was created for them. Twelve district Home Loan banks were established to make loans to S&Ls for liquidity and housing finance needs, and the Federal Home Loan Bank Board was established in Washington, D.C., to regulate S&Ls and to supervise and coordinate the activities of the twelve district Home Loan banks. Membership in

13. Federal charters were not made available for mutual savings banks; insurance, and the federal regulation that accompanied it, was optional to state-chartered savings banks.

the Federal Home Loan Bank System was made mandatory for federally chartered S&Ls and optional for state-chartered institutions.

The Home Owners Loan Act of 1933 charged the Federal Home Loan Bank System with responsibility for promoting activities of S&Ls to improve and increase housing finance. Encouraging and enabling S&Ls to be the preeminent suppliers of housing finance and regulating them in a manner consistent with this aim did much to correct the housing crisis of the 1930s. Unfortunately, the new policies and programs sowed the seeds for the industry's crisis in the late 1980s.

Changes in Banking after the New Deal Reforms

For over thirty years, the New Deal reforms accomplished their mission: the banking industry was stable and profitable, and banks grew substantially. Problems began to develop in the 1960s, however, as market conditions and technological developments eroded the barriers that had kept competitors out; bank profitability fell and instability surfaced. The erosion has continued and accelerated, undermining the efficacy of the New Deal approach and leading to the difficult situation that banks face today.

The New Deal reforms achieved a notable transformation of banking during the remainder of the 1930s. Although the economy bottomed out in 1933, recovery was not complete until full-scale war mobilization began in 1942. But in spite of a weak economy and the poor condition of surviving banks, there were no more financial panics and relatively few banks failed. Only 315 failed from 1934 to 1939, a minuscule figure compared to the 9,000-plus banks that failed in 1933. Those banks that did fail were small.

The depression ended with World War II, and in the subsequent economic boom banks played a major role as financial intermediaries. Much of the public's rising savings was deposited in bank accounts, and banks used these funds to purchase government bonds that financed much of the war effort. By war's end, banking had grown considerably, with most of the growth mirrored in holdings of government securities.

Following a rapid and remarkably smooth transition to peacetime production, the nation began the postwar era in great financial shape. Private debt was very low compared to gross national product (GNP), and banks were safe; over 65 percent of bank assets was in cash and government securities. This allowed the banking industry room to expand quickly, fueling the postwar economic surge by providing an essential source of credit to business. Loan growth came both from expansion in deposits and from restructuring of bank portfolios from cash and government securities to loans. By 1965, the total assets of the banking system were 2.5 times larger than in 1946, and the ratio of loans to total assets had risen from 35 percent in 1946 to nearly 60 percent.

In spite of the rapid growth and portfolio restructuring, bank failures remained rare, averaging under five per year from 1946 to 1965. Earnings more than covered loan losses, allowing banks to accumulate additional equity capital through retained earnings; banks also added to their equity positions by issuing additional stock.

The extremely low failure rate reflected in large part the high degree of protection accorded banks by the government. Restrictions on competition through barriers to entry of new banks, branching restrictions, and limits on deposit interest rates made survival easy for almost any bank. Fraud rather than the rigors of competition was almost always the cause of failure. The public, Congress, and the regulators were lulled into concluding that the New Deal reforms had permanently rendered banking safe and virtually immune to failure. When barriers to competition subsequently crumbled, events revealed that this conclusion was wrong.

Two additional factors contributed to bank stability and profitability before the mid-1960s. Market interest rates and economic conditions were quite stable, particularly in relation to what was to follow. Interest rate ceilings did not interfere with banks' ability to attract deposits, and they were able to earn a profitable spread between their loan income and deposit costs. Market interest rates did drift upward, but when they moved above the ceiling rates for bank deposits and there was a danger that customers might make withdrawals in search of higher returns, the regulators made small, upward adjustments in the ceilings to allow banks to continue to attract funds.

Growth in the thrift industry was even more impressive than for banks. In 1946, total assets held by thrifts were only equal to about 20 percent of the assets held in banks. By 1965, total thrift assets had risen to nearly 60 percent of the assets in the banking industry. Thrifts had become a major element in the nation's financial system. The character of the thrift industry also changed dramatically. In 1946, mutual savings banks dominated the industry accounting for 64 percent of thrift industry assets, with S&Ls holding the remaining 36 percent. Strong demand for housing and government programs to use S&Ls to finance homes eventually made S&Ls the major type of thrift, accounting for 65 percent of thrift industry assets by 1965. During this period of rapid growth, the savings and loan industry also changed from a collection of relatively small mutual associations to an industry dominated by large stockholder companies. The industry came to have only a faint resemblance to the cooperative building and loan associations of the nineteenth century or even to the S&Ls of the 1930s.

The period up to 1965 was also one of increasing competition between banks and thrifts. As household incomes grew and the demand for financial services expanded, banks offered more attractive consumer accounts and loans in direct competition with thrifts. In 1946, banks had only 7 percent of their assets invested in home mortgages and other types of consumer lending, but by 1965 the share had risen to 37 percent. This shift by banks toward serving consumers was to continue, increasing the competitive pressure on thrifts.

The year 1966 marks the turning point for banking—the breaching of the wall between banking and the rest of the financial community. Inflationary pressures had developed because of high government spending on the Vietnam War. Politicians wanted this to be a "costless" war, so taxes were not increased to finance it and interest rates were kept from rising rapidly. The result was a rising quantity of money and excess demand in the economy. Fearing rapidly accelerating inflation, the Federal Reserve broke with its passive policy of moderating swings in market interest rates and tightened money, engineering a sharp increase in interest rates. Banking was hit hard on two sides. Deposit interest rate ceilings were not raised, and as market interest rates rose above the ceilings many customers withdrew funds to invest in Treasury bills and other market instruments; at the same time, businesses increased their demand for bank loans. This produced the credit crunch of 1966.

Banks had informal agreements to grant loans to valued business customers, but the loss of deposits made it difficult to meet these commitments. Most banks met their lending obligations by selling liquid assets and refusing to grant new loans or renew old loans to less valued customers. Others were simply unable to meet their loan obligations. The adjustments were painful for banks and their business customers.

Before 1966, thrifts had no ceilings on deposit interest rates and had most of their funds invested in fixed-rate mortgage loans. Fearing that competition among them would raise deposit interest rates and, therefore, costs, but with no appreciable increase in revenues, thrifts successfully lobbied to have ceilings imposed on them. The interest rate ceilings for thrifts and banks cost both funds as customers made withdrawals for investment in Treasury bills and other securities. With reduced deposits, banks and thrifts had to reduce their asset holdings commensurately, and the entire deposit and asset shrinkage was accorded the clumsy label "disintermediation." With a reduced deposit base, banks and thrifts had to decrease their activities as financial intermediaries. This reduction caused hardship for the businesses and households that relied on depository institutions for credit.

The turmoil produced by the credit crunch of 1966 was so great that the Federal Reserve backed off; it eased up on monetary policy. The subsequent decline in market interest rates induced a flow of funds back into banks and thrifts ("reintermediation").

But the credit crunch had produced a fundamental change in the financial environment. Until the crunch, major corporations had been heavy users of banks as sources of short-term credit to finance their accounts receivable, inventories, and temporary liquidity needs. With this credit source no longer assured, large corporate borrowers began to look elsewhere for funding and found it in the commercial paper market. Commercial paper is short-term, unsecured debt sold in an organized market to corporations, state and local governments, pension funds, and wealthy individuals. Highly liquid because of its short maturity and secondary market salability, commercial paper had been relatively insignificant after the 1920s. Since then, but before 1966, it was used primarily by finance companies as a means of raising funds to underwrite consumer loans. Following the credit crunch of 1966, many other large businesses, including both financial and nonfinancial corporations, began to tap the commercial paper market as an alternative to bank loans. The market grew by 50 percent in 1966 and by 1969 had expanded 250 percent over 1965 levels. And as the commercial paper market grew, many large depositors learned that they did not need to place short-term funds in bank deposits but could instead invest directly in low-risk commercial paper, which paid a substantially higher return.

The growth of the commercial paper market was the first of many developments that broke down the barriers separating banking from the rest of the financial community. The intermediary service offered by banks was simply not worth it to many large borrowers. Prime commercial lending, the traditional bread and butter of banking, was slipping away.

Large banks did not sit idly back and watch their major corporate customers leave. Realizing that their problem stemmed from the inability to raise funds to meet their customers' loan demands, banks developed their own means of using financial markets. Large banks worked diligently to develop the market for their negotiable certificates of deposit. These are deposits in name only. In reality, these CDs are short-term debt instruments (securities) sold by banks in an organized market.[14] The negotiability feature provides CDs with high liquidity; they can be sold in a secondary market before maturity. Negotiable CDs have a minimum denomination of $100,000, but they are typically sold in $1 million lots and were designed to be competitive with Treasury bills, commercial paper, and other money market instruments that were enticing large depositors away from banks. With negotiable CDs, banks themselves breached the dam between banking and financial markets.

But regulators tried to keep the barriers intact by declaring negotiable CDs subject to interest rate ceilings. This meant that negotiable CDs could not be competitive with other money market instruments when market interest rates rose above the ceiling. As long as the ceiling prevailed, banks could not use negotiable CDs as a means of raising funds when depositors deserted them.

A second credit crunch in 1969 provoked responses by large banks that permanently destroyed the divisions segmenting the financial system. In an effort to reverse the increasing inflationary pressures caused by escalating U.S. involvement in the Vietnam War, the Federal Reserve again pursued a restrictive policy that pushed interest rates up sharply. Market interest rates rose above deposit ceiling rates and disintermediation recurred. With negotiable CDs subject to the ceiling, large banks now used Eurodollars (dollar deposits in offshore branches and affiliates) and commercial paper of bank holding companies to circumvent the problem.

Large American banks had operated branches and affiliates overseas for many years. These offshore entities often maintained accounts and offered loans in the currency of the host country, dealing with both U.S. companies doing business in that country and local residents. But they also made available dollar-denominated accounts and loans. This was done because international transactions were commonly conducted in dollars. Both U.S. banks operating overseas and foreign banks issued liabilities and granted loans denominated in American dollars, with much of this activity, particularly in the 1960s and 1970s, concentrated in London. The dollar-denominated bank liabilities and loans were part

14. They should not be confused with consumer CDs, which have smaller denominations and cannot be sold before maturity.

of the Eurodollar market.[15] Because this dollar market was situated in a foreign country, it was beyond the reach of the U.S. government and its bank regulators.[16] The British government took little interest in regulating it as long as transactions were conducted in dollars.

Until 1969, the Eurodollar market was largely independent of the domestic activities of American banks; it was primarily a vehicle for international trade and finance. Now, however, U.S. banks borrowed huge amounts of dollars in London, paying the market rate of interest, and transferred the funds home to be used for domestic lending. American banking regulators lacked the authority to regulate interest rates in London, so they could not stop the practice. The resulting explosion in the size of the Eurodollar market ended the substantial isolation of the United States from international financial markets. A close interdependency, continuing to this day, was established as large U.S. banks became "internationalized." Large banks also circumvented interest rate ceilings and raised funds through the commercial paper market. They formed corporations called one-bank holding companies whose only asset was the stock of the bank. A holding company, which is legally not a bank and whose liabilities are not subject to interest rate ceilings for bank accounts, issued commercial paper paying competitive interest rates. The funds raised in this way were transferred to the bank to support lending. Thus, large banks found a way to use the commercial paper market to their advantage rather than simply watch it siphon off their best customers.

Confronted with the reality of the situation, banking regulators capitulated in 1970 and suspended the interest rate ceiling on negotiable CDs, enabling large banks to add another means of raising funds, even when market interest rates were high. Now armed with negotiable CDs, Eurodebt (deposits and debt instruments issued offshore), and commercial paper, large banks had full flexibility to borrow in both the domestic and foreign money markets. Just as the effects of taxing bank notes had been thwarted in the 1860s by the growth of demand deposits, the effects of interest rate ceilings were thwarted in the 1960s by the movement of large banks into the money markets. In both cases, banks

15. Today there are active dollar markets in many countries, including those in Asia, but the term "Eurodollar" is still used to denote dollar-denominated deposits issued by banks or branches outside the United States.

16. Among other things, this isolation protected such countries as the Soviet Union from the possibility that their dollar deposits could be seized by the U.S. government. Such a possibility would exist if they held deposits with banks located in the United States.

found ways to break down an artificial barrier erected by the government.

The exodus of major corporations from banks to the commercial paper market and the introduction by large banks of methods to tap the national and international money markets were the beginning of a revolution that dismantled the protective structures erected by the New Deal banking reforms. Although the credit crunches of 1966 and 1969 were the catalysts, underlying economic and technological forces would inevitably have doomed the old system.

As rising inflation produced higher interest rates, both lenders and borrowers became more attentive; simultaneously, new technology allowed them to do a better job of managing their financial positions. From today's perspective of powerful personal and microcomputers, incredible mainframe computers, sophisticated data bases and software, and satellite communications, it is easy to lose sight of how recent the computer and information revolutions are. In the 1960s, computers were much more expensive and primitive. But they were the first generation of machines that had widespread, practical business use, and they allowed both banks and their corporate customers to automate their routine activities, setting the stage for a massive shift to new technology in nearly all areas of finance in coming years.

During the 1960s, automation allowed large corporations, state and local governments, pension funds, and universities to consolidate, centralize, and monitor their cash-management activities to a degree previously impossible. Customers with cash in excess of current needs began to seek out short-term investments rather than keeping the funds idle in banks. Rising interest rates provided the economic incentive, and computers made active management of cash positions feasible. For these large customers, the interest return from holding short-term money market instruments was greater than the costs of actively managing their cash positions, so they shifted excess funds from noninterest-bearing bank checking accounts to U.S. Treasury bills and high-grade commercial paper. As a result, major customers came to use banks less extensively as depositories, becoming direct lenders themselves in the money market.

On the other side of the market, corporate borrowers discovered that computers dramatically reduced the costs of borrowing directly from surplus units, defined previously as anyone with income or wealth in excess of current needs. The centralization and close monitoring of cash flows allowed corporate treasurers to do a much better job of anticipating needs for short-term credit, which further enabled them to tailor specific debt instruments (commercial paper) that they could make available to surplus units.

But what about the information and monitoring problems involved in having surplus units evaluate the riskiness of engaging in direct lending? Again computers made a huge contribution. Thanks to the Securities Acts of the 1930s, major publicly traded corporations were already required to disclose a great deal of information about their profitability, equity positions, and other relevant data. With the advent of computers, it was possible to assemble data bases using information from disclosure statements and other sources. These data bases made it far easier to assess the risks of extending credit to individual firms and to compare the risk of lending to one rather than another. Private agencies such as Moody's or Standard and Poor's rated the quality of various short-term borrowers, providing expertise in evaluating credit. Individual surplus units did not need to be experts in the activities of borrowers; rating agencies supplied much of the necessary information. In addition, most prime borrowers were already well known and had large equity positions and a history of successful operations. Furthermore, because commercial paper is short-term debt—typically 30–180 days to maturity—purchasers gave up little liquidity when purchasing it. Secondary markets provided even more liquidity prior to maturity, and the specific liquidity needs of large purchasers could be met through private placements in which the maturities of the obligations were tailored to the requirements of the lenders.

Advances in computers, data bases, statistical analysis, and communications lowered the costs of issuing and purchasing commercial paper to the point where banks found it difficult to compete profitably. Banks had to pay interest rates on their negotiable CDs and Eurodollar liabilities that were close to the interest rates on commercial paper, so it became difficult for them to provide loans profitably to their largest corporate customers. Their role as financial intermediaries largely disappeared as far as meeting the repetitive, standard borrowing needs of this important group of customers.

But banks have continued to supply large amounts of tailor-made credit to their major corporate customers. For example, they provide very short-term loans with maturities ranging from overnight to fewer than thirty days, and they extend credit with maturities longer than those available in the commercial paper market. Banks also provide loans whose interest rates are tied, or indexed, to various market interest rates, such as LIBOR (London interbank offering rate) or banks' "prime" rate. They even lend in one currency and have repayment in that or some other currency. The basic point, however, is that banks have been able to keep their major customers only to the extent that they have something to sell that is better than what can be provided by market instruments; meanwhile, they have lost highly standardized forms of credit.

The computer revolution also profoundly affected bank operations. During the 1960s banks introduced computerized accounting for their deposits and loans, along with electronic check clearing. Automation not only cut costs tremendously but also provided information about deposits and loans on a much more timely basis.

Most important, by 1970 improved technology had enabled large banks to transform themselves from passive deposit gatherers, depending on local customers for funds, into active fund-raisers around the globe. It is difficult to overstate the significance of this development for banking and for bank regulation.

Once these banks and parent holding companies gained access to the money markets by issuing negotiable CDs, commercial paper, and Eurodollars, they could directly determine the size of their operations by managing their liabilities. If a bank wanted to grow, it issued more debt in money markets, using the funds to grant more loans and engage in other activities. If a bank wanted to shrink, it reduced its liabilities by not replacing maturing money market debt while letting some of its loans run off.

With managed liabilities, a bank could support a volume of lending and other activities that far exceeded its local deposits. Banks in areas with strong loan demand could provide loans even when their local sources of funding were inadequate. This enhanced economic efficiency by encouraging funds to flow into the areas of greatest need. But large banks were not limited to lending in local markets. Armed with the ability to raise funds at will, these banks developed vast networks for providing loans, arranging equipment leases, and offering other services for their customers. Aided by computer and telecommunications technology, major banks established offices in all the larger U.S. cities,[17] as well as branch and subsidiary networks throughout the world. Further, they frequently joined loan syndications. The activities of large banks were a far cry from the passive depository and lending functions envisaged by the New Deal reformers.

17. By using loan production offices, leasing firms, and other devices, a large bank and its parent holding company could skirt the prohibition against interstate branching.

Although these activities increased the efficiency and flexibility of the banking system, they also carried the potential for serious problems. Liability management, good in moderation, can create disaster if taken to excess. With enormous markets to draw upon, large banks could grow rapidly. Overly quick growth could endanger the stability of these banks because there were (and are) few natural forces to keep the process under control. The root of the problem lay with federal protection for bank liabilities, which allowed large banks to raise vast amounts of funds without having to pay a substantial interest rate premium. One of the natural impediments to rapid growth—rising interest rates—was blunted for large banks.

In order to expand their loans, fast-growing banks may take on more risk, not so much from consciously lending to riskier customers but from losing control over risk management. A rapidly expanding bank can be overwhelmed by its volume of business, finding it increasingly difficult to evaluate and manage the risk it is assuming. Furthermore, it is all too easy to underestimate the risks in order to justify growth objectives. Loan losses rarely occur right away, so a fast-growing bank may be lulled into neglecting the accumulating risk, and by the time losses hit in force, it is generally too late.

Another damaging element in rapid growth is increasing leverage. There is incentive when there is government protection of liabilities to attempt to raise the return on equity by increasing loans and liabilities while keeping equity capital (net worth) unchanged. This is leverage. A simple example illustrates the point. Suppose a bank has $1 billion of assets. It supports these assets with $900 million of deposits and $100 million of stockholders' equity capital, giving a capital-asset ratio of 10 percent. Further suppose that after deducting its deposit interest costs and operating expenses, the bank earns a net income of $10 million for the year. The $1 billion of assets generates $10 million of income for a rate of return on assets of 1 percent. But the bank's owners have leveraged their $100 million investment into $1 billion of assets, yielding a net income of $10 million, or a 10 percent return on equity.

Increasing leverage can be a powerful method of raising the return on equity if a bank does not have to pay a significant risk premium on its additional liabilities. Suppose the bank in the example issues $1 billion of additional negotiable CDs, doubling its size to $2 billion. With equity unchanged, the capital-asset ratio falls from 10 percent to 5 percent. If the bank earns a net income of 1 percent on the new assets, the return on equity rises from 10 percent to 20 percent. In reality, the bank may have to pay somewhat higher interest rates for its CDs because of its heavy liabilities and may have to make concessions on loan interest rates that reduce the return on assets below 1 percent, but to a point the return on equity will tend to rise as leverage increases.[18] If several banks are pursuing the same strategy, however, returns on loans and other activities may be (and in fact were) competed down to the point where there is no increase in the return on equity.

Increased leverage also raises risk. The lower the capital-asset ratio and the higher the leverage, the smaller is the cushion provided by bank equity capital; large loan losses or other unfavorable events can then threaten bank solvency. With federal protection of bank deposits, CD holders and other depositors do not bear the risk; it is shouldered by the FDIC. Furthermore, when leverage is high, relatively small changes in the return on assets result in large fluctuations in the return on equity. With high and rising leverage, the stock of large banks ceased being a "blue-chip," low-risk investment. These banks found it difficult to attract even investors more tolerant of risk because, despite high leverage, they could not offer a high rate of return.

The substantial increase in leverage allowed by government-protected managed liabilities would have raised bank risk even if the quality of assets had remained the same. But asset quality fell, compounding the problem. As major corporate borrowers shifted to the commercial paper market, banks lost out on much of their low-risk lending. Unable to compete profitably against the commercial paper market, banks sought out new sources of business, most of which were more risky than lending to major corporations. Some of the expansion was in loans to smaller businesses—so-called middle-market borrowers—and some was in greatly expanded consumer lending. But much involved more exotic products. Large banks made massive amounts of loans to less developed countries in the 1970s; they became major lessors of equipment ranging from computers to railroad cars to oil tankers; and they became heavy participants in foreign securities and currency exchange markets, transforming themselves into multinational firms.

The rapid growth of large banks and their holding companies led to a flurry of competition among them for the various forms of business they were developing. Rates of return on these activities were driven down so far that they were often not sufficient to compensate for the risks

18. In the absence of government protection, the purchasers of the bank's CDs would insist on an interest rate premium to compensate for the greater risk of default. This would prevent the return on equity from rising and eliminate the incentive for the bank to increase its leverage.

involved. Risks increased because of the rise in leverage and the pursuit of intrinsically riskier activities. Nevertheless, the return on equity for major banks and bank holding companies did not rise despite the approximate 50 percent decline in their capital-asset ratios between 1965 and 1975. This condition has resulted in dire consequences: huge loan losses, eroded earnings and capital, and even outright failure.

The rapid growth and rising leverage made possible by managed liabilities also opened banks up to the risk of liquidity problems. The money markets in which negotiable CDs and other managed liabilities are offered are extremely tough; investors have no loyalty or concern for the institutions that offer their paper for sale. Corporate treasurers, state and local governments, wealthy individuals, foreign investors, and others who purchase the highly liquid, short-term investments traded in the money markets are concerned about yield, liquidity, and risk but not about ongoing banking relations.[19] When investors become concerned that a bank may be in trouble, they may refuse to buy its paper if they are unsure that the FDIC will bail them out. At that point, if the bank offers to pay higher interest rates on newly issued money market instruments, the situation might actually worsen because the higher interest rates may be interpreted by potential creditors as evidence that the bank is indeed in trouble. With conventional creditors unavailable, the bank can place only very short-term liabilities and it has to pay sharply higher interest rates to lenders willing to bear the risk.

A bank that relies heavily on managed liabilities can find itself in a position where it cannot roll over its liabilities except at short-term maturities and high interest rates. When managed liabilities become "unmanageable," a bank may suffer a liquidity squeeze of major proportions. Substantial loan losses, other unfavorable news, or even just a rumor of problems can lead conventional investors to refuse to roll over its maturing debt, creating what amounts to a run staged by the bank's uninsured depositors. It may be possible to replace the lost funds, but only at very short maturities and by paying very high interest rates. This run is slower than a 1930s-type run because funds leave the bank only as the managed liabilities mature, but many of these obligations have short maturities, so a sizable amount matures in just a few days. The run is also "silent"; creditors do not line up demanding cash but receive payment by check or wire transfer to be placed elsewhere.

19. Holders of "core deposits" are often completely covered by deposit insurance; those who exceed the insurance maximum are concerned about their ongoing banking relationship and are unlikely to lose faith at the first sign of trouble.

A bank that supports itself with the "hot money" of the national and international money markets can ill afford a loss of confidence. But the situation is not as precarious as it might appear, because a solvent bank experiencing liquidity problems from a silent run can borrow from the Federal Reserve.[20] Once its crisis is over, the bank can raise funds again and pay off its debt at the Fed. The availability of loans from the Federal Reserve helps stabilize the situation for a bank experiencing a silent run, but it also gives perverse incentives to banks and their creditors to use managed liabilities even more. Because banks know that Federal Reserve loans are available, they can be less concerned about the consequences of silent runs. Creditors are also more willing to provide funds because they know that a silent run will not bring down a solvent bank.

In sum, as large banks slipped out of the protective cover provided by New Deal legislation, the intense competition in many markets made it increasingly difficult for these banks to earn returns commensurate with risks. They came to support over half their assets with managed liabilities; and with increased leverage, the cushion provided by bank equity diminished, exposing them to increased risks from loan losses and other sources.

Strains on large banks surfaced during the difficult years of 1974 and 1975. In 1974, OPEC (the Organization of Petroleum Exporting Countries) quadrupled the price of oil following its highly destructive boycott of petroleum exports to the United States and other countries sympathetic to the plight of Israel. Double-digit inflation, followed by the deepest recession since World War II, hit the nation. The intensity of the recession coupled with distortions created by soaring prices of energy and other commodities quickened the pace of business bankruptcies. Smaller banks and thrifts had to curtail lending as the sharp rise of market interest rates above deposit ceiling rates fueled disintermediation. The largest banks, by contrast, experienced massive inflows of funds deposited by OPEC countries. These banks profitably "recycled" much of the money deposited by OPEC nations by lending to the foreign banks, businesses, and governments that were scrambling to come up with the dollars needed to buy oil. Banks practically fell over each other to lend large sums to capital-hungry LDCs. These recycling

20. Superficially, this was the situation faced by Franklin National Bank in 1974, Continental Illinois in 1985, and First Republic Bancorp in 1988. But these banks were insolvent even in the absence of a liquidity squeeze. Problems of illiquid but solvent banks receive little notoriety because they are handled quietly by the Federal Reserve. Loans by the Federal Reserve to large insolvent banks will be discussed in chapter 4.

efforts, endorsed by government officials, further increased leverage at large banks.

In spite of the boon to the largest U.S. banks from the inflow of OPEC money, not all large banks were immune to failure. The most celebrated failure was of the multibillion-dollar Franklin National Bank of New York in 1974. This failure and the way the Federal Reserve and FDIC dealt with it are discussed later. For now, it is sufficient to note that the demise of Franklin National is an excellent example of what can happen when a bank grows too rapidly.

Until the 1980s, smaller banks and thrifts could not use managed liabilities. With minimum denominations of $100,000, negotiable CDs were not a viable instrument; for similar reasons neither was Eurodebt. Dependent on their local deposit bases, smaller banks and thrifts had limited leverage, but local deposits fluctuated widely. As market interest rates moved above and below deposit interest rate ceilings, these institutions were subject to waves of disintermediation and reintermediation. Because their supply of available credit moved in concert with their deposits, smaller banks and thrifts faced a competitive disadvantage against large banks, whose access to the money markets allowed them to make loans consistently available.

By the mid-1970s, banks and thrifts also faced the new threat of money market mutual funds, which, by opening the money market to small savers, were to alter fundamentally the competitive environment and ultimately induce elimination of deposit interest rate ceilings for all banks and thrifts. Money market mutual funds signaled the arrival of a new generation of financial institution that could provide many of the conventional functions of banks with greater efficiency and less need for regulation. In many respects, they could outperform banks in providing just those services that were at the core of banking: checking accounts and loans to prime commercial borrowers. Given their importance, it is worth describing why they originated and how they operate.

Money market funds became an important element in the financial system because ordinary households were getting a raw deal on their accounts at banks and thrifts. Interest rate ceilings were kept at such low levels on these accounts that they often failed to earn a return sufficient to offset inflation. In terms of purchasing power, customers were suffering losses. By providing ordinary households a means of purchasing money market instruments indirectly and thus earning a reasonable rate of return, money market funds offered a way out.

Money market funds offer accounts to the public that are technically shares in a mutual fund, but they look and work like a bank account. The money "deposited" in the accounts is pooled and invested in such money market instruments as Treasury bills, commercial paper, and banks' negotiable CDs. After a management fee is deducted, the interest income on the money market instruments is paid to the accounts on a *pro rata* basis. Account holders can treat their accounts much like checking accounts in a bank. Checks can be written against them, and wire transfers are often available.[21] Many money market funds initially had minimum check sizes of $250 to $500, but this practice has largely disappeared.

A money market fund is a financial intermediary whose functions are quite similar to a bank's. Both money market funds and banks offer accounts that are payable on demand, and they invest the funds deposited with them in assets that customers typically could not or would not acquire on their own. They differ fundamentally, however, in the types of assets acquired, the extent to which they are regulated, and the availability of federal insurance.

As mentioned in chapter 2, banks' deposit liabilities are largely backed by illiquid loans. This makes them vulnerable to runs and liquidity crises, which necessitate the federal safety net and heavy regulation. In contrast, money market funds back their deposits with highly liquid and safe assets. High liquidity is achieved by investing in readily marketable instruments with short maturities, typically 30–180 days. There is a much better match than exists for banks between the liquidity of assets and the accounts that are used to fund them. This matching was not available when banks were invented. The development of huge markets for money market instruments has obviated the need to back demand obligations with illiquid loans.

In spite of the low risk and high liquidity of assets purchased by money market funds, their accounts are not as safe an option as a bank account. When funds are deposited with a bank, federal deposit insurance guarantees a depositor with an account balance of $100,000 or less that the full amount will be repaid. Further, larger depositors can be virtually certain that the safety net will be used to protect them. Money market funds have neither federal insurance nor a safety net for their liabilities, and they present a real, though small, risk to their holders.

Consider default risk. Some money market funds invest only in U.S. Treasury securities, which have no risk of default. Other money market funds invest in high-grade commercial paper and in negotiable CDs

21. Check clearing and wire transfers are done by a bank, which earns a fee for this service. Money market funds cannot perform these services directly because they are prevented by the Federal Reserve from doing so.

issued by major banks; defaults are rare for these assets. Furthermore, these money market funds are highly diversified: they spread their investments across many different issuers of commercial paper and CDs. Failure of any one or even several would be unlikely to undermine the ability of a money market fund to meet its obligations.

Money market funds also encounter risk from changes in the prices of the assets they hold. If market interest rates rise, the prices of the assets in a money fund's portfolio decline in recognition that they pay less than newly issued instruments. This means that the value of a money fund's asset portfolio declines. The decline is temporary, however, because as the assets mature, the money is reinvested at the higher interest rate. But in principle, the temporary decline could be sufficiently great that the fund could not repay customers the full amount they put in. Though this possibility exists, it is remote because of accumulated interest and because the prices of short-term instruments are not very responsive to changes in market interest rates. Still, the value of assets held by a money market fund could fall sufficiently to prevent it from redeeming its shares at par. This would not put the money fund in default, however, because it is not obligated to redeem shares at par; legally, the shares are stock, not debt.[22]

What about liquidity risk? Money market funds operate much like banks in the sense that on any given day some customers are making withdrawals and other customers are making deposits. The inflows and outflows are offsetting, and the net change in a fund's total liabilities tends to be small. There is, however, the danger that customers will lose faith and stage a run. Here the difference from banks is striking because money market funds, in contrast to banks, hold their assets in highly liquid, marketable securities. They can meet withdrawals by using money from the sizable amount of securities maturing on any day and by selling their Treasury bills, commercial paper, and negotiable CDs. These sales can be completed in a matter of minutes. It is conceivable that if a number of money market funds experienced runs at the same time, the massive sales of money market instruments would so depress asset prices as to prevent the money funds from repaying at par, but this is improbable. If a general panic did occur, the Federal Reserve, through open-market purchases of securities, can prevent a collapse of asset prices, cushioning the decline in the value of money market fund shares.

22. In practice, operators of money market funds use their own capital to maintain the value of the funds when a decline in asset values would otherwise preclude payment at par. They do this to make their money market fund more attractive to the public but are not required by law to do so.

Finally, there is always the danger of fraud. Some employee of a money market fund might skip the country with a chunk of the fund's assets. Money market funds do not have the FDIC to fall back on to offset these losses.

One is left with the conclusion that accounts at money market funds are much like those of banks, except for some small risk. But the risk is much smaller than would be the case for bank accounts in the absence of insurance. By extending insurance to them, money market accounts could be made safe with little need for additional regulation or supervision.[23] This possibility is discussed in chapter 5.

Two sets of circumstances led to the creation of money market funds, one economic and the other technological. The economic incentive was produced by market interest rates that rose far above the interest rate ceilings set for banks and thrifts, offering an opportunity to attract small depositors away from depository institutions. At the same time, advances in computer, communications, and accounting technology allowed money market funds to purchase and sell assets and to keep track of their customers' deposits and withdrawals at low cost. Fund managers could earn handsome fee incomes while still offering small investors a decent rate of return.

The growth of money market funds was like a laboratory experiment showing how arbitrary regulatory constraints are circumvented in a market economy. They allowed smaller depositors to circumvent interest rate ceilings. Money market funds became major purchasers of the commercial paper issued by large corporations that were deserting banks as a source of funds. Small savers through money market funds ended up financing the borrowing of these businesses.[24]

It is important to stress what the money market funds accomplished. In effect, they took over a substantial portion of the historical monetary and lending functions of banks. On the monetary side, they provided the public with accounts payable on demand, permitting check writing and wire transfers. On the loan side, money market funds lent to prime corporate borrowers through the commercial paper market. Money market mutual funds were in essence banks that fell outside the legal definition.

23. Money market funds are currently regulated by the Securities and Exchange Commission, which establishes standards for the quality of assets purchased and sets minimum diversification requirements, along with rules for accounting practices and disclosure.

24. Pension funds and other institutional investors also came to be major users of money market mutual funds.

By 1980 some $275 billion was invested in money market funds. The drain of funds from smaller banks and thrifts caused such havoc that these institutions reversed their long-held pleas for protection and began to push actively for deregulation of deposit interest rates. Small depositors had won!

Congress at last began the gradual deregulation of interest rates on the accounts offered by banks and thrifts in 1980, completing the process by 1985. Furthermore, in recognition of the weak competitive position of thrifts and their statutory inability to diversify, Congress allowed them to offer checking accounts and to engage in consumer lending outside of the housing area.

These efforts were insufficient to end disintermediation, and in 1982 Congress acted again by deregulating the interest rates on banks' and thrifts' consumer checking accounts and authorizing a new money market deposit account to be competitive with those issued by money market funds. Congress also recognized that S&Ls needed to diversity further and achieve a better balance between the maturity of their assets and liabilities. The investment powers of thrifts were extended to include commercial lending, so that their investment powers became much like banks', and in some areas, such as real estate development and acquisition of low-quality corporate debt, they were given greater freedom than the banks. Banks received no new investment powers.

With deregulation of deposit interest rates, small banks and thrifts could compete with the money market for funds. Smaller institutions no longer had to depend upon their local economies for funds; they joined the large banks in the liability management businesses.

It might appear that smaller institutions faced a considerable disadvantage in raising funds because they lacked the size and recognition to allow them to issue negotiable CDs. Here again markets sprang up to solve the problem. Stockbrokers and others gathered up funds from their customers situated all over the country and delivered them to institutions willing to pay a favorable interest rate on their accounts. These customers did not have to be concerned about safety because each account was kept at or below the $100,000 limit, providing the protection of federal insurance. Small customers had a single account; larger ones had their funds distributed among a number of institutions to obtain total insurance protection. These brokered accounts allowed small banks and thrifts to compete actively and effectively for funds.

With the development of brokered accounts, smaller banks and thrifts acquired much the same flexibility in setting leverage and achieving rapid growth as was available to large banks. Many small institutions—particularly thrifts—quickly became large ones, and many managed to get themselves into trouble. The temptations were particularly great for thrifts, because they operated in a more lax regulatory environment than banks and because recent legislation allowed them to engage in a number of new and profitable, but risky, activities. Many used their huge quantities of insured, brokered deposits to acquire low-grade corporate bonds (so-called junk bonds), engage in real estate development, and finance other unusually risky ventures. The demise of scores of thrifts that followed is grim testimony to the penalties of giving in to the temptations of liability management and to the failure of the thrifts' regulators to anticipate and control escalating risks.

The serious problems banks and thrifts encountered actually had their origins in the late 1970s, before much deregulation had occurred. In 1979, with inflation reaccelerating and a commodity boom under way, OPEC engineered huge increases in the price of oil; inflation soared into double digits. Credit expanded rapidly as large banks recycled the increased flow of petrodollars, and both large and small banks substantially increased their domestic lending in the booming areas of energy, agriculture, and real estate. With high and rising values of the property and other assets backing their loans, banks apparently felt well protected. In short, there was a great deal of borrowing and lending based on speculation that high rates of inflation were here to stay.

Loans to developing nations again expanded sharply, particularly to Latin America. At the time, banks considered these loans to be low-risk. Mexico was sitting on vast oil reserves; Brazil was undergoing an economic miracle of high growth; and with agricultural and commodity prices rising worldwide, banks applied the same logic to other Latin American, Asian, and African countries. Armed with huge financial resources provided by the swollen flow of petrodollars and buoyed by optimistic forecasts of world economic conditions and hopes of becoming the bankers for newly emerging economic powers, large U.S. banks lent foreign borrowers vast amounts of money at highly favorable terms. The very low spread between banks' cost of funds and lending rates point to both the rosy view they had of foreign borrowers and the strong competition to get in on the ground floor.

Beginning in the latter part of 1979, monetary policy shifted to unprecedented severity. Interest rates soared to record levels, and economic activity fell worldwide. The United States plunged into the worst recession since the 1930s, and business and personal bankruptcies rose sharply. With the market for their exports declining and interest charges on their floating rate loans at extremely high levels, borrowers in many LDCs found it increasingly difficult to make payments on the huge amount of debt that they had accumulated.

In spite of the economic distress, the Federal Reserve, determined to bring down inflation, kept the heat on interest rates. The process turned out to be more protracted than anyone anticipated. Even though unemployment was rising and markets were collapsing, inflation fell only a little to begin with, but then the reduction—"disinflation," as it came to be called—intensified. In 1980, consumer prices had risen 13.5 percent, and in 1981 they rose an additional 10.4 percent; but inflation decelerated to 6.1 percent in 1982 and 3.2 percent in 1983.

The disinflation produced staggering problems for banks and many of their borrowers. Energy prices, along with agricultural and other commodity prices, actually declined, disproving the inflationary expectations that lay behind the outstanding loans. With slowing or declining prices, borrowers' revenues were not sufficient to cover the payments of interest and principal; it became increasingly difficult for many domestic and foreign borrowers to repay their debts. In 1982, prompted by an imminent crisis when the LDCs found themselves unable to make loan payments, the Fed finally eased up on monetary policy. But by the end of 1982, loan defaults and bank failures were on the rise, and the thrift industry faced disaster.

From 1982 to late 1990, the U.S. economy enjoyed continued economic expansion; inflation remained relatively low, while unemployment fell. In spite of this impressive economic performance, the situation for the banking industry managed to go from bad to worse. Bank failures increased dramatically during the years 1982–88, with each year setting a new post-1933 record, and as the economy dipped into recession in late 1990, bank failures accelerated. Thrifts did even worse; scores failed, the thrift insurance fund became insolvent, and the federal government in 1989 began a costly program to clean up the mess.

If current problems are to be corrected and future ones avoided, we need to determine why there have been so many bank and thrift failures despite years of economic expansion and general prosperity. In understanding bank failures it is important to distinguish between immediate causes that tip an institution into failure and the fundamental economic forces that made banks vulnerable in the first place. The ultimate cause of the weakened banking system is the disappearance of the barriers that had protected banks from much of the competition they now face.

The growth of nonbank financial conglomerates exemplifies the extent to which banking's protective barriers have been breached. Beginning in the late 1970s and accelerating in the 1980s, financial conglomerates were formed that offered many of the same services as banking organizations, but because these conglomerates did not own banks, they escaped the statutory and regulatory restrictions imposed on banks and bank holding companies. Conglomerates offered monetary services through money market funds, along with stock and bond funds, brokerage services, securities underwriting, real estate brokerage, insurance, and many other financial services, all under common ownership and control. These financial supermarkets were established by such financial firms as Merrill Lynch and American Express, such insurance companies as Aetna, such retailers as Sears and J. C. Penney, and even such manufacturers as General Motors, General Electric, Ford, and Gulf and Western.[25]

Money market funds offered one means for financial and commercial firms to offer monetary services, but operation of thrifts was a widely used alternative. The law allows any company to own and operate thrifts; for example, Merrill Lynch, Sears, and Ford own thrifts. This was not very important until deregulation allowed thrifts to offer checking accounts, commercial loans, and consumer loans, transforming them into a convenient vehicle for outsiders to enter banking.

As mentioned earlier, erosion of traditional markets and declining profitability induced banks to seek out new customers and, exploiting FDIC protection of their uninsured deposits, to increase leverage. During the 1970s, they had been heavy lenders to agriculture, energy, real estate, and LDCs. These were the areas hardest hit by the worldwide recession of the early 1980s, and in many cases these sectors failed to share in the economic expansion that followed. Depressed energy prices were a boon to consumers but spelled disaster for energy firms in Texas, Oklahoma, and Louisiana, as well as for oil-exporting LDCs such as Mexico. The same is true for low farm prices. Domestic farmers in the Midwest and other agricultural regions failed in record numbers, and LDCs such as Brazil received depressed prices for exports of their crops. Furthermore, real estate in the United States was hard hit during the recession. Though it recovered in some parts of the country, it became even more depressed in energy- or agriculture-dependent areas of the country like Texas.

Problems of this sort affected small and large banks alike. Although small banks have been immune to the LDC situation, many were devastated by depressions in energy, agriculture, and local real estate. The

25. For a full list, see Litan, *What Should Banks Do?* pp. 114–17.

most celebrated large bank failure was the demise of Continental Illinois of Chicago. Here the problem was primarily the result of too rapid growth and an inability to assess loan risk properly. It is important to stress this fact because some reports mistakenly associated the failure of Continental with deregulation of deposit interest rates. Continental was a wholesale bank that did not rely on consumer accounts. Like other wholesale banks, it had been paying market interest rates for years. Its basic problem was that it made an incredible number of bad loans. Similarly, the failure of the banks of First Republic Bancorp and of MCorp, both of Dallas, in 1988 and 1989 demonstrated the dangers of concentrating loans in a state dependent on high energy prices.

Although banks have made progress in writing off and otherwise disposing of substantial amounts of LDC debt, huge quantities remain on their books. The continuing saga of near defaults on LDC loans has received well-deserved notoriety because of the massive amount of lending, the prominence of the lenders—the largest banks in the country—and the political-diplomatic issues posed by these problem loans. Though losses on these loans have not brought down any of the big banks yet, the threat of massive defaults by LDCs remains a major source of concern.

Banking is clearly not the safe, highly profitable business it once was. But when one considers the size of the shocks and imbalances, the smallness of the equity cushion, and the heavy reliance on managed liabilities it is impressive that most banks have weathered the storm so well. Most banks are, in fact, very good at controlling risk. Far and away the largest number of failed institutions have been small banks in the farm and energy belts where the inability to diversify spelled disaster. But banks are in a far weaker position today than they were at the beginning of the 1980s. Another major economic downturn could cause an upheaval that both regulators and the FDIC would be ill-equipped to handle.

For the thrift industry, disaster occurred early. This book is not the place to discuss in detail the S&L debacle, but some lessons emerge from it that are relevant to banking. In assessing what happened to S&Ls, it is important to realize that much of the industry had been in serious difficulty for years. With the emergence of competing lenders and the need to pay market interest rates for deposits, the profitability of mortgage lending declined. In addition, S&Ls faced interest rate risk because of a huge imbalance between the maturity of their assets and liabilities: when interest rates rose sharply, many S&Ls became unprofitable because the costs of their liabilities increased quickly, whereas the income from fixed-rate mortgage loans rose only slowly. During the late 1970s and early 1980s, when interest rates shot up to unparalleled heights, losses were widespread. When interest rates subsequently fell, many returned to profitability, but meanwhile there had been a huge erosion in equity positions. Many institutions, particularly in energy-producing states, suffered large defaults on their loans and started to use brokered deposits in an effort to grow their way out of adversity.

Congress recognized that the industry's problems arose in part because it was forced to be overspecialized. It was believed that by allowing S&Ls new powers to engage in consumer and business lending, greater diversification and better balance between maturities of assets and liabilities could be achieved, enhancing stability and ultimately the ability to provide housing finance. Unfortunately, matters did not work out this way for much of the industry. Congress overreacted by giving S&Ls powers to engage in activities deemed too risky for banks, and states commonly granted even wider powers for institutions under their jurisdiction. But more important, institutions were not supervised in what they did. Rather than moving cautiously into new activities, many raced in with abandon, using brokered deposits to fuel ferocious growth. Fraudulent activities increased markedly in this environment. Even if the new powers of S&Ls had been limited to exclude real estate development and junk bonds, there was ample scope for getting into trouble.

Part of the problem lay with the structure of and approach to S&L regulation. Supervision had historically been fairly straightforward because the business of S&Ls was relatively simple—accepting deposits from local customers and dispensing home mortgage loans. When interest rate risk surfaced and expanded investment powers were granted, regulators were ill-prepared to meet the new challenge. Supervisory staffs were insufficient, and the attitude of regulators was still attuned to encouraging industry expansion rather than counseling prudence.

To this regulatory environment we must add the perverse incentives created by small capital positions at many institutions. Stockholder equity was at very low levels (often negative when measured in terms of market values of assets), providing a powerful temptation to engage in high-risk ventures with a high potential payoff. The logic is clear: stockholders had little to lose if the activities were not successful and a great deal to gain if they were. Not surprisingly, most of these efforts were unsuccessful. High-risk ventures became endemic, and scores of thrifts became insolvent as they saw their interest rate speculation, real estate development activities, junk bonds, and other gambles go bad.

Institutions were able to get away with taking such risks because their regulators were not vigilant and depositors were willing to provide the funds necessary to support dicey activities because deposit insurance protected them from loss. In fact, depositors often sought out the most venturesome S&Ls since these institutions were paying premium interest rates on their brokered deposits. The situation got out of control because for many S&Ls there was no entity, private or public, restricting risk taking.

Matters turned from bad to worse after the mid-1980s as S&L insolvencies soared. The FSLIC, the agency charged with insuring S&L deposits, suffered massive losses from protecting depositors at failed S&Ls. The insurance fund began to run out of money, so the FSLIC raised insurance premiums in an effort to generate more funds. But high premiums would tend to tip weak S&Ls into insolvency and worsen losses to the insurance fund. The Reagan administration and Congress were unwilling to provide much assistance, in part because fiscal rescue measures would worsen the budget deficit. The FSLIC was encouraged to limit payouts from the insurance fund by looking the other way when institutions became insolvent, allowing them to continue operation in the hope that matters would improve. But this only further increased incentives to take risks because stockholders at insolvent S&Ls had nothing to lose and depositors were still insured. The FSLIC worked frantically to find ways to stop the hemorrhaging while avoiding payouts since it was broke. Mergers were arranged in which the acquiring entity was guaranteed against losses, subjecting the FSLIC to large payments in the future but saving it from current spending. Congress authorized special tax write-offs to acquiring institutions, subjecting even the U.S. Treasury to lost future revenues to spare the FSLIC. These delay maneuvers simply compounded an already desperate situation.

Finally, the Bush administration, after taking office in 1989, moved aggressively to stop the bleeding and to reform regulation of the thrift industry. The result was the Financial Institutions Reform, Recovery, and Enforcement Act of 1989 (FIRREA). The legislation authorized a massive bailout of the government's S&L insurance program. Funds were authorized to shut down more than five hundred insolvent S&Ls, paying off insured depositors and liquidating the institutions' assets. At present, the cost of the operation, including interest on debt issued to provide financing, is estimated to be $300–$500 billion. Some of the funding will come from higher insurance premiums for S&Ls, but most will come from debt issued directly and indirectly by the federal government. The interest and principal will ultimately be shouldered by taxpayers.

FIRREA did much more than shut down insolvent S&Ls; it also reorganized and strengthened insurance and regulation for S&Ls. The FSLIC was eliminated and its insurance and regulatory duties shifted to the FDIC, which now operates separate insurance funds for "savings associations" (federal- and state-chartered S&Ls and federally chartered savings banks) and for banks. The Federal Home Loan Bank Board was eliminated, and the Federal Home Loan banks were stripped of their regulatory and supervisory duties. The Office of Thrift Supervision was established within the U.S. Treasury to be the primary regulator and supervisor of all federally insured savings associations. Both the Office of Thrift Supervision and the FDIC regulate and supervise federally insured savings associations, but FIRREA gives the FDIC final say.

Regulation was also tightened. S&Ls and other savings associations were subjected to meaningful capital requirements—after a transition they will end up the same as those imposed on national banks—savings associations lost the authority to invest in junk bonds, and the powers of state-chartered institutions were reduced to match those of federal savings associations.

FIRREA also refocused national housing finance programs. Federal Home Loan banks were devoted to raising funds in the market and lending to member institutions for the purpose of providing housing finance. Eligibility for loans was expanded beyond savings associations to include commercial banks, credit unions, and insurance companies, provided they have at least 10 percent of their assets in residential mortgage loans and meet certain other criteria. Furthermore, institutions with at least 70 percent of their assets in housing-related loans become "qualified thrift lenders" and receive preferential treatment in obtaining loans from Federal Home Loan banks.

Savings associations that fail to meet the criteria for qualified thrift lenders must either become national banks or be regulated exactly like national banks. In effect, the new act requires savings associations to stick to housing finance if they are to receive special treatment. It is by no means clear that this effort to force S&Ls and other savings institutions to specialize in housing finance will permit them to thrive. Huge continuing losses by thrifts suggest that much of the industry will fail. Recall that it was specialized institutions that experienced the declining profit margins and interest rate perils in the late 1970s and early 1980s that triggered the S&L crisis in the first place. But at least now institutions have an out: they can convert to national banks if a broader range of services is required to assure their viability.

Although much of the industry is in terrible shape, there have always been many conservatively managed, profitable thrifts. Most of these institutions used their expanded powers sparingly and wisely, sticking primarily to the kinds of business they knew best. Unfortunately, these institutions now suffer because high-risk thrifts have pushed up deposit interest costs and insurance premiums for everybody. They also have to labor under the deteriorating reputation of the industry they represent.

It is also important to realize that FIRREA was designed only for S&Ls, trying imperfectly to clean up their mess and subjecting savings associations to the same quality of regulation as banks. But banks have not fared so well themselves. Nothing in the act addresses the problems that face all depository institutions.

Modern Banking

Although it encountered major difficulties, banking never approached the collapse experienced by thrifts. Apart from having been subjected to tougher regulation, banks have been far more successful at adapting to the changing financial environment. Banks and bank holding companies have not stood still as competition from financial conglomerates has increased and conventional loan markets have slipped away. They entered as many new activities as the law allowed, while greatly expanding others. The Federal Reserve—the regulator of bank holding companies—aided the process by lengthening its list of permissible activities for bank holding companies. Banks and their holding company affiliates do direct placements of corporate securities and have begun to underwrite these securities on a limited basis. They underwrite commercial paper. They provide full-scale investment and merchant banking overseas and brokerage services domestically. They guarantee the commercial paper of corporate customers and the debt of states and municipalities; and they "securitize" consumer, mortgage, and some business loans, insuring, underwriting, and selling the securities backed by these loans in the market. In many ways the large banks and bank holding companies of today are financial conglomerates themselves. The lines between banking and other financial organizations are becoming hopelessly blurred.

But in the process of adapting to the changing environment, the character of banking has changed fundamentally from the days of the

New Deal reforms. Banking organizations have evolved into financial services firms with a wide range of activities in which monetary services and provision of highly specialized credit to borrowers constitute a relatively small and shrinking part. Yet concern for monetary services and credit provision is what led to the heavy regulation and sheltering of banks from competition to begin with. Why continue to protect entire banking organizations in order to protect these two elements?

To see the limited degree to which banks' activities involve provision of monetary and specialized credit services, let us check the balance sheets of banks' assets and liabilities. If we look at the major asset categories for the U.S. banking industry, in terms of aggregate dollar amounts and as a percentage of total assets, we see that the absolute dollar figures are huge, totaling over $3 trillion of assets (table 3.1). About a third of these holdings are devoted to cash and marketable securities, but 62 percent are in loans and 6 percent in such other assets as bank buildings. These figures indicate that banks do indeed devote most of their assets to loans.

But what kind of loans? Let us break down bank loans into major categories (table 3.2). Only 30 percent of all bank loans are to commercial and industrial borrowers. Of the $3 trillion-plus of assets held by banks, only $609 billion, or 18 percent, are devoted to the kind of business lending that historically made banks special. Even this figure overstates the degree to which banks deal in loans where their expertise in evaluating and monitoring risk comes into play. Billions of dollars of these commercial and industrial loans are very short-term and other special credits to major corporate borrowers who find it convenient to borrow for certain purposes from banks. Banks are competitive in these areas not because of their lending expertise—little is required in evaluating an overnight loan for AT&T or IBM—but rather because the

Table 3.1

Commercial Bank Assets: Domestic and Foreign Offices, December 31, 1989

	Billions of dollars	Percentage of total assets
Cash and securities	1,050	32
Loans	2,029	62
Other assets	205	6
Total assets	3,284	100

Source: Board of Governors of the Federal Reserve System

Table 3.2

Commercial Bank Loans: Domestic and Foreign Offices,
December 31, 1989

	Billions of dollars	Percentage of total loans	Percentage of total assets
Commercial and industrial	609	30	18
Real estate	750	37	23
Consumer	382	19	12
All other	288	14	9
Total	2,029	100	62

Source: Board of Governors of the Federal Reserve System

government's safety net allows them to borrow at a relatively low cost for this kind of lending. Furthermore, loans to finance leveraged buyouts, loans to LDCs, and many other kinds of activities far removed from a bank's historic functions are included in the figures for commercial and industrial loans. Business lending involving the kind of information gathering and monitoring that made banks unique and important is a small part of what they now do.

The other kinds of lending—real estate, consumer, and so forth—are important but not unique to banks. Real estate loans account for a larger share of total lending than do commercial and industrial loans. Much real estate lending is for home mortgages, which are available from a variety of sources. The rest is primarily for construction and acquisition of office and apartment buildings; the presence of insurance companies and other lenders demonstrates that banks have no special expertise here either. Banks are also major lenders to consumers through both credit cards and financing for the purchase of cars and other major items. Again, banks are not unique in this field; many other institutions offer consumer credit.

Add in banks' financial services that do not involve the issuance of liabilities and acquisition of assets, such as securities underwriting and placement, and credit guarantees; as in other categories, here they are only one set of players among many. Why should banks' extension of credit and of financial services receive the support of the federal safety net when other financial firms, which are not protected, provide in many cases exactly the same kinds of loans and services?

One area in which banks' activities are unique and vital is in furnishing loans to businesses too small to use securities markets. Banks have special expertise in assessing and monitoring such projects. One would not want this service to disappear, but it is probably less than 10 percent of what the banking industry does. Is it really necessary to protect and regulate the other 90 percent of bank activities to assure provision of this credit?

It is true that only banks (and thrifts) offer insured liabilities payable on demand and are part of the payments system, but this is because the government has granted them a monopoly. Does provision of these monetary services merit the protection and heavy regulation of banks and thrifts? Most bank liabilities are not payable on demand, and most are unrelated to the payments system. Attempts to safeguard monetary liabilities by protecting banks brings a huge volume of nonmonetary liabilities under the government's protective umbrella. Surely it is not necessary to regulate and protect entire banking organizations just to ensure that their monetary services are safe. As we shall see in the final chapter, it is perfectly feasible to separate banks' monetary functions from their other activities.

Finally, what about banking's sources of funds (table 3.3)? The figures are shown both in absolute dollar amounts and as a percentage of total funds (which equal total assets). The first item is the aggregate of all checking and savings accounts in the banking industry, the most global definition of accounts that either are or could be payable on demand. Though over $1 trillion, these constitute only 37 percent of all sources of funds. The largest source is time accounts and other nonmonetary liabilities ranging in maturity from thirty days or less to many years. They include individuals' time accounts, but most are negotiable CDs, Eurodebt, and other liabilities issued in the national and international financial markets. In total, these nonmonetary liabilities account for 57 percent of all sources of funds. The remaining 6 percent is stockholder equity.

Table 3.3

Bank Liabilities and Equity: Domestic and Foreign Offices, December 31, 1989

	Billions of dollars	Percentage of total assets
Checking and savings accounts	1,205	37
Time accounts and other liabilities	1,875	57
Equity	204	6
Total	3,284	100

Source: Board of Governors of the Federal Reserve System

We saw in chapter 2 that banks historically filled a void as financial intermediaries, taking "positions" by issuing liabilities (deposits) to surplus units while holding loans extended to deficit units. But rising income and wealth, technological improvements that lowered the costs of information and transactions, development of new market instruments, and improved financial education have made it far easier for surplus units to deal more directly with deficit units. Banks (and thrifts) are needed less and less as position takers.

The reduced need has been slow to reveal itself because the safety net allows banks to issue liabilities that are essentially risk-free to surplus units while holding the risky loans granted to deficit units. In spite of the hidden subsidy in federal protection of their liabilities, banks have found it increasingly difficult to compete. We saw that the first real threat came from the commercial paper market, but the corporate bond market and other financial vehicles have subsequently expanded their presence as well.

Mutual funds have made significant inroads by offering the public effective means of holding claims on stocks, bonds, and other debt instruments issued by business. Mutual funds offer both relatively low risk, thanks to diversified portfolios, and a high degree of liquidity— shares can be liquidated quickly, often by check or telephone. Improved technology and advances in financial management have allowed a wide variety of mutual funds to develop, ranging from money market funds to bond and stock funds with various risk-return features to combinations of several funds. It is possible today for even a relatively small saver to invest in the money market, in the bond market or stock market, or in any combination of these. Mutual funds are replacing banks as a vehicle for shifting financial resources from surplus to deficit units, a process that will doubtlessly continue over the long run in spite of the advantage provided banks by the shield of the safety net. The inroads that mutual funds have already made indicate clearly that this advantage is far from limitless.

Realizing that their role as position takers is diminishing, banks have moved increasingly into other kinds of financial services, becoming less "banklike" and more like other purveyors of financial services. Banks have been most successful in areas where they have been able to exploit their expertise, technological efficiencies, and information advantages.

In managing their asset and liability positions, banks have developed sophisticated methods for hedging the risks of unexpected changes in interest rates and foreign exchange rates by using markets in which interest rate futures contracts and forward contracts for foreign exchange are traded. These markets allow banks to purchase and sell securities or foreign exchange in the future at the interest rate or foreign exchange rate prevailing at the time the contract is purchased or sold. Futures and forward markets permit banks to pursue strategies to control their interest rate and foreign exchange rate risk, and many now market these strategies to various customers in return for fees. Interest rate and foreign exchange "swaps" have also greatly expanded. An S&L with long-term, fixed-rate mortgages financed by short-term deposits may be interested in exchanging (swapping) the fixed income from its mortgages for an income stream that better matches its liability costs. Similarly, some business holding assets whose income is denominated in Japanese yen may be interested in swapping with some other business whose assets yield income in French francs or U.S. dollars. Large banks typically put together such deals and operate as dealers in swaps, earning substantial fee income.

Another area that banks have moved into aggressively is investment banking. This has taken fullest form overseas, where banks have complete investment banking powers, but it is also pursued in the United States. Banks are engaged actively in direct placements of various securities because this activity is not covered by the Glass-Steagall restrictions and the Federal Reserve has ruled that bank holding companies can underwrite and deal in securities on a limited basis without violating these restrictions. In many cases, banks are able to combine their detailed knowledge of issuers of securities with knowledge of the needs of clients who may be interested in buying the securities. In all these activities they bring surplus and deficit units together directly without themselves taking positions that intermediate between these two groups.

Banks are also shedding their role as position-taking intermediaries by "securitizing" their assets—converting loans they have granted into securities that are sold in markets. In effect, securitization transforms assets that are difficult to sell into highly marketable securities. This conversion process bridges the gap between borrowers and investors; banks are not position takers with loans financed by liabilities but rather creators of securities.

Securitization takes many forms, but the importance of the process can be seen in the highly developed area of mortgage loans. By using automated credit rating agencies; by establishing standards for income level, job tenure, and down payments required for loan approvals; and by using uniform standards for property appraisals, lenders have been able to achieve high volumes of mortgage loan activity at low cost. The heightened uniformity has made it easier for those who originate the loans to sell them to someone else. Given knowledge of the standards applied in granting the loans, potential purchasers are able to evaluate the risks involved. Uniform standards transform what used to be private information available only to lender and borrower into information that is easily communicated to outsiders. This is a revolutionary change because mortgage loans no longer need to be held by those who originate them; lenders no longer need to be position takers issuing liabilities to fund portfolios of mortgage loans.

Once uniformity of mortgage loans was achieved, it was a relatively small step to transform these loans into securities. This swelled the mortgage market by reducing risk and increasing liquidity. Banks, thrifts, and others originate many mortgage loans during the course of their business. When a sufficiently large number are accumulated, they are packaged together and transferred into a trust. Securities are then issued backed by the mortgages in the trust. They are called mortgage-backed bonds and have several advantages over holding mortgages directly. All of the bookkeeping and payment flows are consolidated in the payments of interest and principal on the bonds. Furthermore, because each bond is backed, on a *pro rata* basis, by many mortgage loans, the holder receives the benefit of substantial diversification. Risks are further reduced by various forms of insurance provided by the issuers of the bonds. And because the bonds are uniform, they can be traded in an organized market, providing the holder with substantial liquidity.

Securitization has allowed banks and thrifts to earn fee income for originating, servicing, and insuring mortgage loans while selling them to others. The attractiveness of this activity is exemplified by the rapid growth of competing institutions called mortgage banks that perform these services without ever accepting deposits or holding mortgage loans for investment purposes. They borrow short term (often from banks) and sell the mortgages they originate. Their success is direct evidence that it is not necessary to be a position-taking depository institution to grant and service mortgage loans. It is in the *holding* of these loans for investment purposes that depositories historically played a role.

Securitization makes it possible for mortgage loans to be held indirectly by pension funds, mutual funds, individuals, and depository institutions. A single loan to an individual household, secured by an individual home, ends up as part of a bond that trades in an active market. High technology made this revolution possible by drastically reducing the costs of keeping track of all the components, but human ingenuity led to standardization and the idea of backing bonds by mortgage loans.

The economic role of banks and thrifts in mortgage lending has changed dramatically. To be sure, their expertise in lending and their considerable skills in automation are still highly valuable, and they continue to originate and service loans. But they no longer obtain any natural advantage in actually holding the mortgages. Banks and thrifts no longer need to finance holdings of twenty-year mortgage loans by issuing six-month deposit certificates. Pension funds, mutual funds, and others are quite willing to add these long-term instruments to their portfolios. This drastically lessens what banks, and more importantly thrifts, contribute as holders of mortgage loans. Thrifts are in fact becoming obsolete; the difficulties that so many have encountered are no accident. Thrifts have much to contribute as mortgage banks but little or nothing as position takers. Government deposit insurance is what keeps so many mortgage loans in the thrift industry.

Following the lead offered by mortgage-backed bonds, banks have been working diligently at finding ways to securitize other assets. Consumer loans show considerable promise. As with mortgage lending, banks have established automated procedures for processing and granting these loans. Again, credit history, income, and job tenure are important factors. The procedures used can be communicated to and confirmed by outsiders, providing the basis for securitization. Banks have begun to issue securities backed by car loans and even unsecured credit card debt. The market for these shorter-term instruments is still developing, and standards are still being worked out; one major problem is that unlike mortgage loans there is no uniform standard concerning the default risk that is accepted by consumer loan originators. Some banks concentrate on relatively low-risk consumer loans, while others are willing to accept greater risk and the higher interest rates that go with it. With time, more uniform standards will likely evolve, and banks will routinely issue securities backed by these loans.

Business loans, especially those that are unsecured, are often the most difficult to securitize, since detailed ongoing information about each borrower is usually required to evaluate and control loan risk. Although banks have considerable expertise in evaluating these loans, it is often tough for them to communicate the information in a credible manner to outsiders; verification is difficult. Banks have been successful, however, in selling an impressive amount of business loans. Loans to major corporations—and even to lesser businesses when information about the character of the loans and condition of borrowers can be reliably communicated—are marketed. Sales of business loans have been aided by bank practices in two ways. First, some banks devote substantial resources to originating, servicing, and selling these loans. This not only gives them expertise in coming up with marketable loan products, but also signals purchasers of the loan sellers' commitment to the process as an ongoing business, enhancing sellers' reputations for trustworthiness. Second, loan sellers often retain a partial ownership of the loans they originate and service, which assures purchasers that sellers have a financial interest in originating good loans and carrying out the monitoring required to keep them that way.

So far, most sales of business loans have been made to other banks, typically by large banks to smaller ones. But over time it is likely that many types of business loans can be securitized and sold to nonbank investors like mutual funds. Issues concerning cost and accuracy of communicating information about individual loans, reputation of loan originators, and financial interest retained by loan originators will be important in determining the extent to which securitization of business loans is possible. Despite this potential, many business loans are far too complex and specialized to securitize. For such loans, position taking is justified by the economics of the situation. As we already have seen, however, these loans comprise only a small part of banks' current position taking.

Banks will increasingly channel their expertise, information, and technology into service activities. They will accelerate their efforts at securitization, serving more as loan originators and servicers but less as liability issuers and loan holders. The shift away from position taking to financial services will continue even though the government's safety net subsidizes banks to issue their own protected liabilities to finance asset acquisitions. The potential profits from devoting a major part of bank activities to position taking do not compensate for the risks. Banks that have tried to continue along this path rather than moving into safer and more remunerative activities have suffered. The most successful banks, for the most part, have been making the shift voluntarily.

But the path that banking follows and the role it plays in the future will depend upon the nature and extent of the regulatory restrictions that are imposed by the government. The greater the restraints placed on banking to keep the industry in its historical role, the smaller the amount of financial activity that will be conducted through banks. Clients will move to other, more flexible and less regulated purveyors of financial services, with potentially serious consequences for monetary and financial stability.

4

Bank Regulation and the

Federal Safety Net

Profound changes and stresses are transforming banking and its competitive environment. Although bank regulators have taken some actions to treat the worst symptoms that have emerged from the tranformation, little has been done to deal with fundamental problems. Indeed, the regulatory approach is a major problem preventing banks from adapting to the changing environment.

To set the record straight, the bank regulatory agencies are staffed and run by dedicated and intelligent people who have helped keep banking safe for nearly fifty years following the New Deal reforms. Even now, as the efficacy of these reforms are coming undone, the regulators still contribute. Many banks, particularly smaller ones, are brought under control and induced to behave more prudently. But the press does not celebrate the successes. It is the failures and near failures that receive all the media attention, creating the impression that the regulators can do nothing right. This is certainly far from the truth; yet the efficacy of bank regulation *has* declined considerably. The philosophy of regulation continues to be based on the New Deal approach of protecting banks and separating them from the rest of the financial community, but this approach will no longer work. Bank regulation is sorely outdated, and the results are only too visible.

Who are the regulators and how do they operate? Responsibility for bank regulation on the federal level is divided among three separate but overlapping agencies: the Comptroller of the Currency, the Federal Reserve, and the Federal Deposit Insurance Corporation. It is broadly accurate to say that regulation and supervision of banks and bank holding companies is parceled out as follows: the Comptroller oversees national banks; the FDIC oversees state-chartered banks that are not members of the Federal Reserve System; the Federal Reserve has oversight responsibilities for state-chartered member banks and, more important, bank holding companies, which include (with certain exceptions) all companies that own or control banks with insured deposits. This apparatus is made more complex by a bewildering array of overlapping jurisdictions, perhaps the most important of which is the centralization of regulatory authority over international operations of all banks in the Federal Reserve. On top of this, each of the fifty states has authority over the banks it charters.

Thrift regulation is also complex. The Financial Institutions Reform, Recovery, and Enforcement Act of 1989 placed primary responsibility for regulating and supervising all insured savings associations and S&L holding companies under the Director of the Office of Thrift Supervision (DOTS), an office established by the act within the U.S. Treasury Department. But the FDIC, which insures thrifts and maintains a separate insurance fund for them, may also examine thrifts, and it is required to prescribe and enforce any regulations that it finds necessary. In enforcing its regulations, the FDIC recommends to DOTS that action be taken, but if it is not forthcoming the FDIC may act directly. Savings associations must meet the same minimum capital requirements as national banks, dictated by the Comptroller of the Currency. In addition, FIRREA subjects S&L holding companies to essentially the same activities as bank holding companies, and these are prescribed by the Federal Reserve Board. Added to the complexity on the federal level, state-chartered thrifts are also under the jurisdiction of state regulatory authorities.

Before discussing important details of bank regulation, let us review the economic rationale behind it. As noted earlier, it was often difficult for depositors to monitor and influence bank behavior. The government, in effect, came to act as agent for bank depositors and other creditors, providing the assessment, monitoring, and control of bank activities that these creditors often either could not or would not do on their own. Several advantages accrued from centralizing these activities in the government. There were obvious economies of scale in policing against fraud and controlling bank risk taking, enabling the supervisory agencies to develop a degree of expertise in banking affairs that was impractical for many creditors. Furthermore, centralization made it easier to establish uniform standards of supervision and monitoring and to obtain information from banks in a consistent manner while retaining confidentiality for bank customers. Equally important, the government could impose legal sanctions to force errant banks to stop engaging in activities that were deemed undesirable. In the absence of this direct regulation, depositors could force compliance with their wishes only by taking their business elsewhere, or at least threatening to do so.

When government participation in bank regulation began, disclosure of relevant data by banks about their operations was weak and of questionable reliability. The government exerted its legal authority to force disclosure of reliable data on banking affairs. Unfortunately, government regulators also developed the tradition of keeping information about the affairs of banks (as opposed to those of their customers) to themselves, making it difficult, even with the aid of computer technology, for private analysts to assess bank performance. But public disclosure of banking affairs has improved recently, and it is no longer obvious that the government has a clear economic advantage over private firms in providing this service. Officials still have access to more and better data than are available to private analysts, the result of retaining bank examiners with clearly defined public responsibilities.

When federal deposit insurance was introduced in 1933, the government became more than just an agent for private depositors, however. With deposit insurance, the government, through the FDIC, became a potential creditor. The FDIC is obligated to provide sufficient funds to pay off insured depositors should a bank fail. This contingent liability gives the government a direct stake in supervising, monitoring, and controlling bank behavior.

Bank Regulation in Practice

Regulatory agencies have both a regulatory and a supervisory function. As regulators they establish rules that interpret and give specificity to the banking statutes. As supervisors they engage in on-site inspections and other information gathering to police conformity with law and regulation.

Although banking laws and regulations are complex, their primary intent is to promote "safe and sound" banking. Regulators follow a prophylactic approach, seeking to circumscribe what banks do. The first step is to define what a commercial bank is. Simply put, an institution, other than a savings association, that accepts deposits insured by the FDIC qualifies as a bank. But what about other activities? The National Bank Act allowed banks to have "all such incidental powers as necessary to carry out the business of banking" and left it to the Comptroller of the Currency to establish these incidental powers. They have been determined to include, among others, certain types of data processing services; leasing, selling, and underwriting of credit-related insurance; operating securities brokerages; and performing certain kinds of investment banking. But general commercial activities; travel services; underwriting or selling of life, health, or casualty insurance; offering real estate brokerages; or engaging in those investment banking and other securities activities prohibited under the Glass-Steagall Act of 1933 have been deemed not to be incidental powers and are therefore prohibited.[1]

Although the restrictions placed on bank activities are intended to promote safety and soundness, it is often difficult to find the logic in allowing some powers and not others. For example, why is it consistent with safety and soundness for banks to offer data processing services and stock brokerage but not travel services and real estate brokerage? Much in existing regulatory standards can be explained better by political expedience than by considerations of bank safety and soundness.

Having delineated a bank's allowable activities, the regulators determined the standards for establishing one. The organizers of a new bank must put up initial equity capital, have experienced management and a sound business plan, and give reasonable assurance that the bank will be viable. Regulator approval is required not only for new banks but also for mergers and acquisitions, formation of bank holding companies, and undertaking of new activities not already permitted. Although these restrictions are intended to promote safety and soundness, it takes little imagination to see how they can be used to reduce competition and innovation.

Restrictions are also imposed on loans and bank capital. Oddly, few restrictions affect direct lending even though loans are major sources of risk that can threaten bank safety and soundness. In order to avoid overconcentration of loans, national banks cannot have loans to a single

1. Many states allow their state-chartered banks to do what national banks can do, though some states allow greater insurance and securities powers for their banks.

borrower or related group of borrowers that exceed 15 percent of the bank's capital, with certain exceptions. For most banks, this translates into having less than 1 percent of assets in these "single" loans. There are also severe restrictions on "insider" loans to bank owners, directors, and officers. Finally, banks may not lend more than 10 percent of capital to a single nonbank affiliate, such as a nonbank subsidiary of the parent holding company, and no more than 20 percent to all such nonbank affiliates. These loans must be fully collateralized, and the transactions have to be at arm's length—that is, use the same standards with respect to interest rates and other factors as apply for loans to nonaffiliated entities.

In the late 1970s, concern over the large decline in bank equity positions, particularly for large banks, led the regulators to impose minimum standards for bank capital in an effort to achieve larger buffers to protect the FDIC, and potentially uninsured depositors and other creditors, against losses. The standards were initially qualitative and flexible, but congressional concern over federal regulatory enforcement of capital standards led in 1980 to a requirement in the International Lending Supervision Act that the regulators establish and enforce minimum levels of capital for the banks under their jurisdiction. The highly specific and rigid capital requirements that resulted are worth discussing in detail because capital requirements have become a key element in regulation and illustrate practical problems faced by trying to regulate today's banks.

Capital requirements invite circumvention. When a simple method was used requiring banks to maintain a minimum ratio of capital to total assets, banks developed ways to meet the letter of the regulation while getting around its spirit. Those that had insufficient capital-to-assets ratios did raise them, but many banks offset the effects, changing the composition of their asset portfolios by reducing their holdings of Treasury securities and other low-risk assets and increasing riskier assets. The higher ratio of capital to assets accomplished little if anything in providing added protection against bank failures.

Another method used to circumvent capital regulation was to take many activities "off balance sheet." An off-balance-sheet item is simply one that is not reported on a bank's balance sheet of assets, liabilities, and capital. For example, if a bank guarantees someone else's loan for a fee, the loan does not appear on the balance sheet and no additional capital is required, but the bank's exposure to loss from loan default is the same as if it had granted the loan in the first place. Loan guarantees became widespread through the use of what are called standby letters of credit. Banks encouraged lesser-known corporations to which they had formerly lent to issue commercial paper backed by these standby letters, and municipalities were encouraged to issue their own debt backed by standby letters of credit. This practice allowed corporations and municipalities to borrow in the market on the strength of the bank's name but obliged the bank to pay off the debt if the borrower defaulted. Through the use of standby letters of credit, banks removed loans from their balance sheets and raised the ratio of capital to assets without experiencing any reduction in risk. They would have had the same risk by simply lending to the corporations and municipalities in the first place and keeping their former capital-asset ratio. This is a clear perversion of capital requirements.

Other forms of off-balance-sheet activities also involve taking on risk without showing assets and liabilities to go with it. For example, banks guarantee interest rate and foreign exchange swaps, operate in futures and options markets, and grant daylight overdrafts (within-day loans). Banks also engage in all sorts of contingency arrangements; a large bank may underwrite short-term debt issued by a major corporation or a foreign government in the Euromarket, promising to provide credit if the customer becomes unable to roll over its debt to other lenders or if the interest rate it has to pay when rolling over the debt exceeds some agreed-upon maximum. All of these activities subject banks to risk of varying degrees but are absent from the balance sheet and therefore circumvent capital requirements.

Regulators responded to these problems by developing an elaborate scheme of risk-based capital requirements to be used in conjunction with overall capital requirements. The risk-based capital adequacy standards, as they are called, are the culmination of negotiations among twelve nations to establish comparable standards for their international banks.[2] Although the standards were designed to provide "competitive equity" for major international banks, the United States has elected to apply the standards to all its banks and, with a few modifications, to their holding companies as well.

The new standards weight various asset categories by their degree of risk. There are four categories. Business and consumer loans are apparently viewed as among the most risky assets because they receive a weight of 100 percent. Revenue bonds issued by states and munici-

2. The standards apply to banks in the United States, Japan, West Germany, Britain, France, Canada, Italy, Sweden, the Netherlands, Belgium, Switzerland, and Luxembourg.

palities and home mortgage loans, including privately issued mortgage-backed securities, are seen as half as risky as business loans, since they receive a weight of 50 percent. Deposits in other banks, general obligation bonds of states and municipalities, and mortgage-backed securities backed by U.S. government–sponsored agencies are reckoned to be 20 percent as chancy as business loans; they receive a weight of 20 percent. Vault cash, reserves held at Federal Reserve banks, U.S. government securities, and debt directly and unconditionally guaranteed by the wealthy countries are apparently deemed to have no risk and receive a weight of 0 percent.

Each asset held by a bank is assigned a risk category. By multiplying the dollar amount of assets in each category by its risk weight and summing the weighted amounts from each category, a total is obtained. Many types of off-balance-sheet activities such as standby letters of credit and interest rate and foreign exchange swaps are assigned a "credit-equivalent" dollar amount and placed in a risk category for appropriate weighting. Standby letters of credit receive a weight of 100 percent, the same as outright loans. The weighted credit-equivalent amounts are added to conventional risk-adjusted assets to get a figure for total risk-adjusted assets.

A minimum capital adequacy standard (requirement) of 8 percent is imposed against total risk-adjusted assets.[3] The new 8 percent capital standard appears to be an increase over the 6 percent (of total unadjusted assets) standard previously imposed and therefore to provide a larger equity cushion to protect the FDIC and deter risk taking, but the comparison is not as simple as it might appear.

For items shown on the books as assets, total risk-adjusted assets are less than total unadjusted assets. Only those items that have a 100 percent weight, such as business and consumer loans, add dollar-for-dollar to risk-adjusted assets. Those with lower weights add less. For example, with their 50 percent weight, each dollar of mortgage loans or municipal revenue bonds gives only 50 cents of risk-adjusted assets. Banks with large amounts of mortgage loans and municipals are actually required to have less capital under the new 8 percent standard than under the old 6 percent standard because their total risk-adjusted assets are much lower than their total unadjusted assets. Other banks, particularly those with substantial holdings of business and consumer loans and those that have large quantities of standby letters of credit outstanding, have experienced increases in the amount of capital they must have.

3. The scheme is being phased in and is scheduled for completion at the end of 1992.

Regulators also defined two tiers of capital. Tier I capital consists of conventional (common stock) equity capital, including loan-loss reserves. Tier II capital includes preferred stock and subordinated debt and can be composed completely of the latter. Up to half of the 8 percent capital requirement may be met by Tier II capital. Thus, banks are allowed to support their total risk-adjusted assets with the equivalent of only 4 percent of risk-adjusted assets as common stock equity; the remaining 4 percent can be subordinated debt.

All of this complexity is enough to make a grown person cry—or laugh if cynically inclined. What reasoning process led the regulators to come up with the items included in each risk category, why four categories, and why were the particular weights chosen and not some others? Why is collateral not taken into account in assigning risk to business loans?[4] How did the regulators conclude that all business loans have the same risk no matter who the borrower or what the maturity? This is what is implied by giving loans to prime corporate borrowers—including, for example, overnight loans to AT&T and IBM—the same 100 percent weight as loans to finance wildcat oil drilling and leveraged buyouts. Furthermore, by what logic are loans to highly capitalized and profitable corporate giants twice as risky as revenue bonds issued by municipal- or state-operated public utilities as implied by the 50 percent weight for revenue bonds? Why is a consumer loan secured by a car twice as risky as a home mortgage loan?

On top of all their problems of complexity and irrationality, risk-based capital standards distort portfolio choices and get in the way of effective risk control by well-managed banks. Under the new scheme, banks have to put up more capital in granting business loans or car loans than they do in granting mortgage loans or purchasing revenue bonds, raising the cost of granting business and car loans relative to these other activities. In addition, no allowance is made in the capital adequacy standards for the principles of asset diversification. Risks are treated as additive. But to impose effective capital requirements the regulators have to be able to measure and evaluate the overall risk faced by each bank. It is necessary not only to assess the risk of each individual activity in which a bank engages, taking all actual and contingent liabilities into account—both on and off the balance sheet—but also to determine how the risks interact. Some risks are offsetting, whereas others reinforce each other. Effective diversification can greatly reduce the aggre-

4. Only loans secured by U.S. government securities are assigned a lower risk category. All other forms of collateral are neglected.

gate risk to a bank of pursuing a number of individually risky activities. Under the risk-based capital standards, there are no rewards for effective diversification and no penalties for ineffective diversification.

The risk-adjusted capital adequacy standards are already distorting and overly complex, and they will probably become even more so over time as the regulators respond to banks' attempts to circumvent them. This unhappy cycle is likely to break down eventually.

Supervision

Regulatory agencies monitor banks to determine if they are operating in accordance with law and regulation, and more generally if they are being managed honestly and prudently. The agencies rely on both direct examinations and periodic reports filed by each bank.

Direct examinations involve on-site inspections in which internal records and management procedures are assessed. Examiners use the CAMEL rating system (Capital, Assets, Management, Earnings, and Liquidity) to gauge a bank's performance in each area and its overall strength. Special effort is devoted to assessing the quality of a bank's loans. Examiners use sampling techniques to ferret out loans that are, or soon will be, in default, as well as those that appear to be unusually risky.

Assessing bank risk goes beyond examining individual loans, however, to even more complex and difficult issues. Examiners consider whether undue concentrations of loans have been granted to borrowers with common vulnerabilities, meaning that they must somehow predict the vulnerabilities. They attempt to determine whether loan interest rates and other charges are commensurate with the risks involved, which requires them to estimate the contribution of a particular type of loan or other activity to a bank's overall risk. Examiners must also evaluate the maturity of a bank's loans and other assets relative to the maturity of its liabilities, the size of its core deposits relative to its managed liabilities, and whether its mix between fixed- and variable-rate loans is consistent with the structure of its liabilities. On top of all this, examiners must determine the extent of a bank's risk of loss from off-balance-sheet activities and then assess the extent to which they contribute to the bank's overall risk. This is particularly tricky because certain important off-balance-sheet activities may actually offset risk incurred elsewhere. Finally, examiners are required to assess bank management. Supervising bank performance is difficult, to put it mildly, and though the problems are perhaps tractable for small banks, they are intractable for the giant multinational banks. In all cases, the judgment of the regulators is pitted against that of bank management.

Supervisory functions are also carried out at the regulators' home offices through analyses of periodic reports on earnings, balance sheets, and other data that banks file. These reports, along with material from direct examinations, are put into data bases that are analyzed by computer to make comparisons among groups of roughly similar banks. These data bases have allowed the regulators to develop "early warning systems" designed to flag potential problems.

Regulating and Supervising Bank Holding Companies

The Bank Holding Company Act, as amended in 1970, applies essentially the same standards for allowable activities of bank holding companies that are applied to banks; they must be "closely related" to banking and must not promote "unsound banking practices." The Board of Governors of the Federal Reserve System is responsible for regulating and supervising bank holding companies, including determining what specific activities are allowable.

The Federal Reserve Board has interpreted restrictions on holding company activities narrowly, for the most part including only those activities that could be performed directly by the bank. It also regulates and supervises holding companies and their nonbank subsidiaries much like banks. The board issues regulations and rulings designed to promote the financial soundness of bank holding companies, inspects the holding companies and their nonbank subsidiaries, and requires frequent reports. Capital requirements, including risk-based capital, are imposed on bank holding companies, and standards of safety and soundness are applied.

The Federal Reserve Board has taken the position that bank holding companies should be a "source of strength" for their subsidiary banks. This apparently means that it wants to assure the safety of bank holding companies so that they can come to the assistance of any subsidiary banks that encounter financial difficulties.

Problems with Bank Regulation

Bank regulation has been and continues to be primarily retrospective. Emphasis is put on inspecting banks' books for how well loans are performing and on evaluating banks' methods for detecting fraud and overzealous employees. By and large, the regulatory agencies react to what has happened rather than anticipate future problems. But a retrospective approach does not suffice in a world where managed liabilities and brokered deposits allow rapid growth, where problems of credit and liquidity risk are paramount, and where banks can move quickly into new, complex financial activities both at home and overseas. Problems can be out of control before they surface in a bank's loan losses or profit performance. Ideally, banking supervisors should spot problems before they get out of control and should instill a degree of conservatism in bankers. In reality, this is asking too much of the regulators.

The regulators are trying to do more than their resources and competence will support. On one level, they try to provide an independent audit function for banks, indicating a justifiable concern over limiting fraud—until recently far and away the largest source of bank failure. Although they can claim some success, it is difficult for these agencies to develop sufficient expertise to unearth subtle forms of deceptive or fraudulent practices. Large banks engage in fantastically complex transactions that are hard to trace and evaluate; in such cases the regulators must depend on a bank's internal management control systems because they lack the resources and expertise to go about the process from scratch.

Consider, for example, congressional investigations into transactions involved in channeling funds from the Iranian arms sales to the Nicaraguan contras. The bewildering array of dummy corporations, payments, and cross-payments made just this one set of transactions extremely difficult to trace despite thousands of hours of work and immunity-induced testimony.

But fraud is only one problem. What about the difficulties of detecting risky activities? This involves a very different kind of audit, full of pitfalls. As we saw in chapter 2, banks are processors and evaluators of private information, and they engage in a vast array of activities, allowing them to take on projects with offsetting risks. To be effective, regulators have to obtain relevant information and evaluate management strategies, an unenviable task.

Government supervisors who interrogate bankers earn maybe sixty thousand dollars a year; the people they question often make ten or twenty times that and operate out of offices that make a regulator's quarters look like a shelter for the homeless. How can regulators second-guess the management of these multinational corporations about the riskiness of a specific loan? Can they evaluate how that loan fits into the entire loan portfolio or how it adds to or deducts from the riskiness of the entire banking organization? How are they going to evaluate the risks of the bank's securities trading, foreign exchange activities, offshore operations, or its bewildering array of off-balance-sheet activities, such as foreign exchange and interest rate swaps? What about hedging strategies using futures and options markets, offshore credit facilities, and so on? The answer is clear: regulators cannot substitute their judgment for a bank manager's, even at a small bank, where dealings are generally easier to track.

What actually occurs is that government supervisors fall back on rules of thumb and historical performance to assess bank risk taking. They compare the record of the bank in question to that of its banking peers. If it is performing about as well as others of comparable size and location, regulators are usually satisfied.

Shifts in management practices and attitudes frequently go undetected, especially if other banks are doing the same; the shifts will not be detected until losses begin to occur. This helps explain why bank lending to LDCs got out of control and why Continental Illinois went so far out on a limb before the regulators reacted.

It seems an inescapable conclusion that regulators are attempting the impossible. There is simply no reason to suppose that, except in extreme cases of management incompetence, they are better at managing a bank than its managers. They lack the expertise and incentives required to do the job Congress has assigned them. The regulatory approach, therefore, must be fundamentally changed. The government must stop trying to police everything related to banking and to prevent all banks from failing. This approach cannot work in today's complex and highly integrated financial environment.

Market discipline should be encouraged as an effective means of reducing the burden on regulators. Let the large, sophisticated investors who buy bank negotiable CDs, Eurodebt, and other money market instruments bear risk along with creditors of bank holding companies. Faced with the possibility of losing their investments, they will police banks out of self-interest. Not all regulation can be left to the market, but a sharing of resources between officialdom and the private sector is bound to be more efficacious than the government acting alone. The ways the market can help will be discussed later, following an analysis of the federal safety net and how it has strayed from its original mission to the point where it inadvertently encourages risk taking by banks and thrifts.

The Federal Safety Net

Nearly sixty years ago, when Congress introduced deposit insurance and converted the Federal Reserve into an effective central bank, it created a safety net that has protected the nation from financial collapse. The efficacy of the safety net is threatened, however, by the technological advances and financial innovations that have integrated domestic and world financial markets. In an effort to guarantee stability in a highly interdependent world, the government has spread the coverage of the net ever wider to more and more activities and markets. But each increase in coverage adds incentive for participants in financial markets to take greater risks in the expectation that the government will bail them out. This in turn has led to more bailouts. The effects are most visible in the problems faced by deposit insurance agencies, but the Federal Reserve's function of providing liquidity has at the same time undergone an unhealthy transmutation to a national policy of bailing out insolvent institutions. What has gone wrong with the safety net, and what attempts have been made to fix it? As we shall see, fundamental changes are needed.

It is important to bear in mind that the original purpose of federal deposit insurance was to guarantee the safety of small depositors' bank accounts, eliminating the incentive for these depositors to stage bank runs and substantially reducing the chance that otherwise solvent institutions would be forced into failure by a liquidity crisis. Coupled with activities of the Federal Reserve to provide liquidity should larger depositors stage runs, the safety net was wondrously successful.

The FDIC resembles an ordinary insurance company in some ways, but insurance premiums are not risk related. Each bank pays the same flat assessment (premium) per dollar of deposits. Premiums are thus more like a tax designed to cover the FDIC's administrative expenses and accumulation of a relatively modest reserve fund. The assessment has never been high enough to provide an insurance fund that totals even 2 percent of all insured deposits.[5] It is possible to get along on such a small insurance reserve without shaking public confidence because the FDIC is not a true insurance company. The insurance fund is

5. The insurance fund as a percentage of total insured deposits has ranged from a high of 1.96 percent in 1941 to a low of about 0.50 percent in 1990. Because the FDIC has adopted a policy of protecting uninsured as well as insured deposits, perhaps it would be more appropriate to calculate the insurance fund as a percentage of total deposits, which would produce even lower figures.

only the first line of defense; if its reserves proved to be inadequate, the FDIC could increase assessments; if this also proved insufficient, it could turn to Congress for assistance, floating debt to cover any additional losses.[6] In effect, insured deposits are backed by the full faith and credit of the U.S. government.

The mere presence of insurance tends to encourage bank risk taking. Before insurance, depositors would, to whatever extent possible, put their money with safe banks. This gave banks a compelling reason to operate prudently in order to attract more deposits. Insurance made all banks safe for small depositors, eliminating the need to shop around for a bank but reducing the incentive for prudent management. In essence, deposit insurance shifted risk from insured depositors to the FDIC. That was one reason the FDIC got involved in bank regulation.

We saw in chapter 3 that bank failures were infrequent until the 1970s, but the FDIC, when dealing with the failures that did occur, adopted procedures that protected uninsured as well as insured depositors; this sowed the seeds for the current difficulties. Actual bank closures and depositor payoffs were, and still are, relatively rare. When a bank fails (or is in trouble and likely to fail), the FDIC's policy has been to arrange a takeover by a solvent bank. This is called a purchase and assumption because the acquiring bank purchases some or all of the failed bank's assets and assumes all of its deposit liabilities.[7] It has the benefit of not disrupting depositors and borrowers at the failed bank— the bank closes one day with one name and set of owners and opens the next with a new name and new owners. It has the deficiency of blunting the incentive for large uninsured depositors to avoid risky banks because they are protected should their bank fail.

Using takeovers to handle failures in the past reduced and often eliminated the claims on the insurance fund. With the severe restrictions then in place on new charters, an existing bank had a high franchise value, so high that the acquiring bank was willing to assume all the liabilities and purchase all the assets of the failing bank and to put up enough capital to have a solvent institution. The FDIC was not out a cent.

6. The FDIC has not yet needed assistance, but the FSLIC received a massive bailout in 1989 before being dissolved into the FDIC.

7. The FDIC may set up a "bridge bank" into which deposits and certain assets are shifted before arranging acquisition by a bank, or it may engage in "open bank assistance," in which the failed bank is kept operating through FDIC capital injections. Though technically different from straight purchases and assumptions, these methods have the same economic effect.

In some cases, the franchise value might not be large enough to attract a suitor, leaving the FDIC the alternative of either closing the bank and paying off insured depositors or subsidizing a takeover by supplying enough capital of its own to make the takeover attractive. The second alternative involved the FDIC's taking over some of the bank's loans or guaranteeing them or simply providing cash, whichever was least expensive to the insurance fund. Because franchise values were high, the FDIC usually subsidized a takeover; about the only banks that actually closed were small, rural ones with low franchise values. The FDIC's procedures benefited customers by keeping the institution in operation.

When the FDIC arranges a takeover, all the troubled bank's depositors end up enjoying protection because the acquiring institution assumes *all* the deposits of the old one. Large uninsured depositors, including holders of large-denomination negotiable CDs and depositors in foreign branches, are protected. But when the FDIC closes a bank, uninsured depositors lose. The FDIC pays off insured depositors and liquidates the bank's assets, sharing the proceeds on a *pro rata* basis with uninsured depositors and general creditors. Since such closures rarely occur, about the only time uninsured depositors lose is when they have funds in relatively small banks that no one wants to buy. By avoiding such institutions, uninsured depositors receive an implicit federal guarantee that their funds are safe. In effect, they enjoy the equivalent of deposit insurance.

In the absence of guarantees, large depositors will insist on a risk premium and ultimately shift their funds if they fear that a bank is too risky. Risk premiums and potential loss of funds penalize banks, thereby encouraging them to shape up. Congress initially recognized the importance of having large depositors at risk when it limited the extent of insurance available to each customer. The FDIC has unfortunately undermined this crucial source of market discipline by pursuing a policy that protects uninsured depositors, and Congress has not encouraged the FDIC to mend its ways. Although purchases and assumptions benefit bank customers by allowing deposit and loan activities of failed banks to continue, and insurance reserves are conserved, at least in the short run, by avoiding depositor payoffs, the costs in terms of increased risk taking by banks and greater burdens on the regulators to control banks are substantial when uninsured depositors are protected. Ultimately, the suspension of market discipline has led to increasing bank failures and huge losses to the insurance fund. We shall presently see, however, that the FDIC can put large depositors at risk while encouraging continuation of services through purchases and assumptions.[8]

Why did it take so long for problems to develop? As long as banks were protected from competition and kept profitable, failing institutions were few and far between. Fraud was really the only way that a bank could be brought down. Deposit interest rate ceilings and high profits kept bank capital ample, at least by today's standards. Banks could not grow very rapidly, and retained earnings allowed capital expansion to keep pace with assets. But everything changed for large banks with the development of managed liabilities and the emergence of nonbank competitors by the end of the 1960s. The integration of these banks with the national and international money markets permitted rapid growth, but profit margins fell and risk taking by many large banks increased markedly.

Uninsured depositors may have expected, but did not know for sure, the extent of their protection until the mid-1970s, when the failure of the large Franklin National Bank demonstrated they had little to fear. A takeover was arranged by the FDIC; uninsured depositors and other creditors of that institution did not lose a cent. Even after that, large depositors and other creditors could not be certain of protection because they might have funds in a bank that was in such sad shape that no one would buy it. This possibility did provide some discipline, and it explains the silent run on Continental Illinois. When the FDIC assumed control over that giant bank, effectively nationalizing it after no takeover could be arranged, what had been implicit policy became explicit. The FDIC flatly promised that no large bank would be allowed to fail. Whatever market discipline had previously existed was further reduced. More and more of the burden of keeping bank risk under control has been shifted to the FDIC, but neither it nor the other regulators can shoulder it.

The discussion up to this point might suggest that the FDIC bears sole responsibility for extending the safety net to cover all bank creditors. In fact, the Federal Reserve has been a willing partner.[9] To see why this is

---

8. The FDIC experimented in the mid-1980s with "modified payoffs" as a means of accomplishing this. With modified payoffs, only the insured deposits and selected assets of a failed bank were transferred to the acquiring bank. Uninsured depositors experienced losses because they only received payments of their *pro rata* claim on remaining assets. The approach had technical flaws, and rather than working to correct them, the FDIC abandoned modified payoffs and reverted to its present policy of protecting uninsured depositors from loss.

9. But not willing to absorb losses in order to protect depositors—that burden has fallen on the FDIC.

the case, we need to review how the Fed and the FDIC interact in their operation of the safety net.

We saw in chapter 3 that in principle the functions of these two government agencies are quite different. The FDIC protects the accounts of insured depositors at insolvent banks whereas the Federal Reserve provides credit to solvent banks when they are caught in a liquidity squeeze. In practice, however, the FDIC and the Fed often act in concert; each is a component in the process that bails out uninsured depositors. If news leaks that a bank is insolvent before the FDIC is able to complete arrangements for some other institution to acquire it, depositors stage a silent run—they withdraw funds when their negotiable CDs and other credit instruments mature. This worsens the bank's condition, making it harder for the FDIC to find a merger candidate and raising the subsidy the FDIC has to offer. If the Federal Reserve did not come to the rescue, the FDIC might be forced to close the bank in order to stop the hemorrhaging, which in turn would inflict losses on uninsured depositors and other creditors. But the Fed does provide assistance by making emergency loans to the insolvent bank. The lost uninsured liabilities are replaced by loans through the Fed's discount window, which keeps the bank afloat. In essence, the Federal Reserve provides liquidity to an insolvent bank, buying the time needed for the FDIC to arrange a takeover. In the process, the FDIC becomes the guarantor of the loans provided by the Fed.

It is important to realize that the Federal Reserve is frequently the leader in the scramble to keep insolvent institutions afloat, particularly if they are large. It needs the FDIC to arrange takeovers and to absorb any losses in the process, as much as the FDIC needs the Fed to provide temporary liquidity. Why does the Federal Reserve want to protect uninsured depositors and other creditors of insolvent banks? Specifically, why did it lend billions of dollars to insolvent banks like Franklin National, Continental Illinois, and First Republic, allowing their uninsured depositors to avoid any losses? One reason is that the Federal Reserve fears that holders of unsecured interbank loans, negotiable CDs, and Eurodollar liabilities of large *solvent* banks would panic and stage (silent) runs if uninsured depositors of large insolvent banks were to suffer losses.

The Federal Reserve apparently views the events surrounding a silent run on an insolvent bank as a crisis that could turn into a 1930s-style banking collapse and financial panic. But if failure of a Continental Illinois or other large bank did panic creditors of solvent banks, the Federal Reserve could use open-market operations to offset any temporary drain of reserves, and solvent institutions losing funds could turn to the Fed's discount window if unable to borrow from private sources. Armed with both loans to solvent banks and open-market operations, the Federal Reserve could stop any banking crisis dead in its tracks without lending to insolvent banks.

If events required, the Federal Reserve would be capable of providing loans and reserves to solvent banks on a massive scale, but in reality it would probably not have to do very much to stabilize the situation. The reason is that silent runs are not massive flights to currency that rob the banking system of reserves, threatening to bring the system crashing down. Rather, they occur when existing holders of a bank's liabilities lose confidence in that bank and demand payment at maturity so that they can reinvest the money elsewhere. "Silent runners" at solvent banks could conceivably elect to hold currency; should this occur, the Federal Reserve is fully capable of replacing the lost reserves. But large currency drains are extremely unlikely because there are safe alternative investments available that unlike currency earn interest. If creditors of solvent banks shift their funds into U.S. banks that are perceived to be stronger, the funds remain in the banking system. Movements of funds from one bank to another cannot cause a banking collapse. The losing banks will attempt to get funds through the interbank market, but if these efforts fail they can turn to the Fed for assistance.

Suppose failure of a major bank caused the silent runners to lose faith in U.S. banks generally and to shift their funds to dollar deposits at foreign banks. Solvent U.S. banks will attempt to borrow in the overseas interbank market and bring the money back home, and with the greater availability of funds at foreign banks they likely will be successful. If not, the Fed can provide assistance. Even if the money were shifted out of dollars and into other currencies, though the value of the dollar might fall in foreign exchange markets, U.S. banks could still borrow dollars.[10]

Finally, if silent runners avoided banks altogether and shifted into government or other securities, the sellers of the securities would still have to put the money someplace. Again, it would end up in banks. The simple fact is that, unless the silent runners shifted into currency, the funds would return to the banking system. As the funds shift around, some temporary problems could develop, and they might be severe for some institutions, requiring Federal Reserve assistance to solvent but illiquid institutions, but these difficulties would be secondary. A bank-

10. To the extent that the Federal Reserve or foreign central banks intervened in foreign exchange markets, likely in the case of a sudden reduction of confidence in U.S. banks and the dollar in general, the exchange rate would not even fall.

ing collapse does not occur just because funds are reshuffled from one set of banks to another or from one market to another.

Even if the difficulties for solvent banks are greater than suggested here, they are highly unlikely to overwhelm the Federal Reserve's capacity to handle liquidity problems that may develop. The Federal Reserve has essentially unlimited resources to make funds available. Fears that failure of a Continental Illinois or other large bank could cause financial collapse seem to be founded on the belief that the Federal Reserve will not fulfill its safety net function of providing emergency liquidity. But it makes no sense to argue that the Fed must make the safety net available to insolvent banks to assuage the fear that it might not spread it under solvent ones.

Nevertheless, the Federal Reserve also props up large, insolvent banks because it fears that failure of a large bank could bring the whole national and international payments system crashing down. In the world of high finance, money whizzes around at a ferocious pace. For the nation as a whole it is estimated that over $1.5 trillion worth of transactions occur during a single business *day*. This is a staggering figure; the total value of transactions during four average business days exceeds a year's GNP. The scope of transactions extends far beyond payment for final output; it includes payments for intermediate goods, transactions in real assets, interbank transfers of funds, securities transactions, and dollar payments in foreign exchange and Eurodollar markets. Over 98 percent of the total dollar value of these transactions is carried out through banks. Most of this volume is not done by checks but by electronic transfers from one bank account to another. During a typical day, a large bank receives thousands of electronic deposits and withdrawals, which tend generally to net out by day's end.[11] A bank's deposit and reserve positions can fluctuate widely during the day; for example, it may have paid out several billion dollars early in the day but not yet received payments from other banks. If these payments materialize before day's end, all is well, but if they do not, the bank can face a liquidity squeeze brought on by a huge decline in its deposits and reserves.

Some basic economic principles help explain why the volume of transactions is so large and why risk develops. At root is the inability to earn interest on certain kinds of balances. Banks are required by law to

11. We focus on the business day because the Federal Reserve settles reserve accounts at the close of each day. Large banks, however, conduct transactions continuously throughout the world and operate, in effect, on a twenty-four-hour basis. Complications raised by continuous trading are not addressed here.

hold reserve balances with the Federal Reserve that earn no interest. These reserve balances must show up in the accounting at the end of each day, but in the meantime banks reduce reserve positions during the day so that the funds can earn income. Banks are also prevented by law from paying interest on demand deposit account balances. In response, corporations and others who must use these accounts do not hold balances any larger than they absolutely have to. With sophisticated computerized cash-management programs it is possible to get along with very slim balances indeed.

Facilitated by sophisticated cash-management systems and electronic funds transfer (EFT), banks and their customers alike have become adept at minimizing the balances held in noninterest-bearing accounts. Funds flow into and out of these accounts almost immediately. In fact, good cash managers often spend funds before they are received. This is accomplished through "daylight" overdrafts, whereby businesses without sufficient funds at the time they want to make payments are given overdrafts (loans) during the day by their banks, to be made up when these firms receive funds later in the day. Daylight overdrafts are off-balance-sheet items because the credit is repaid before the close of business and therefore never shows up on banks' balance sheets, which are calculated as of the close of business. Banks are allowed to draw down their reserve balances at the Fed during the day without paying interest.[12]

If reserve balances earned interest during the day, banks would lose interest income by granting daylight overdrafts and would in turn increase the charges to their customers, making these loans much less attractive to customers. Furthermore, if demand deposit balances earned interest during the day, corporations would not find it attractive to minimize their balances by use of daylight overdrafts and other within-day transactions.[13] In a nutshell, if interest were paid on reserve and demand deposit balances, there would not be over $1.5 trillion worth of transactions on EFT facilities each day, and demand balances in New York City would not turn over an average of nearly four thousand times each year as they currently do.

12. At this writing, the Federal Reserve is considering charging interest for the daylight overdrafts it provides to banks. While the interest rate would be low—amounting to a 0.25 percent annual rate—the Federal Reserve anticipates that it would significantly reduce daylight overdrafts on reserve accounts.

13. With modern computer and communications technology, it is possible to have "real time" monitoring of reserve and demand deposit accounts, and interest accrued by the minute or second.

The huge volume of within-day transactions not only distorts and wastes resources; it also poses risks for individual banks, for the Federal Reserve, and potentially for the banking system. Sending and receiving banks face somewhat different risks. A bank incurs risk when it sends funds for a customer before that customer has sufficient funds in its account to cover the transaction. Though the risks for daylight overdrafts may be low because these loans are so short term, they exist nonetheless.[14] Risk may or may not arise for banks receiving funds. If funds are sent over the Federal Reserve's facilities (Fedwire), there is no risk because the Federal Reserve guarantees the transactions—these funds are fully collected without recourse. If the funds are sent over a privately owned clearing system, however, the receiving bank does face risk. Under CHIPS (Clearing House Interbank Payment System), a private clearing system heavily used for electronic international payments, all transactions are considered conditional until the end of the day.[15] Receiving banks can reduce the balances of customers into whose accounts funds are paid, but the funds rarely stay in the customers' accounts long enough to make any difference. Once the money is spent, the bank has, in effect, extended credit to the customer for the uncollected funds. If the customer cannot or will not make restitution, the bank may sustain a loss or confront the prospect of lengthy and expensive legal action.

A receiving bank using a private system also runs the risk that a sending bank will fail during the day. This is important since large imbalances between cumulative debits and credits often occur during the day as funds are sent back and forth among banks. If a bank that owes substantial clearings fails during the day, the banks that it owes sustain losses.[16] These losses cannot arise for banks owed funds through Fedwire with the Federal Reserve acting as guarantor.

Problems posed by failure during the day of a bank using a private system raise the issue of "systemic risk." The banks owed money by the failing bank could be left in such vulnerable positions that they could

14. Banks often place limits, or caps, on these overdrafts, with on-line approval required for large transactions.
15. On CHIPS, funds are not transferred during the day. Rather, a "sending" bank informs the "receiving" bank of its commitment to deliver funds. At the end of the day, commitments between various pairs of banks are netted and accounts are settled using Fedwire.
16. Users of CHIPS limit risk by establishing bilateral limits on the imbalances that can occur between pairs of banks as well as "debit caps," but risk has certainly not been eliminated.

fail. Unable to settle with banks that they owe, their demise could start a chain reaction to bring the whole system down. Systemic risk arises for banks using a private system such as CHIPS. If a bank, either foreign or domestic, fails and is closed or has its payments blocked before it settles up with other banks, the banks it owes under CHIPS suffer losses that could cause them to fail. Of course, if failed banks are closed after their funds-transfer obligations are met, no problems of systemic risk arise.

Concern over seeing the private electronic payments system, and the large banks with it, collapse like a house of cards when a major bank fails is one of the primary reasons why the Fed engages in emergency bailouts. But the Fed's concerns over systemic risk produced by extensive use of the wire-transfer networks are misplaced; it is extremely unlikely that failure of a major banking participant could bring the system down. To see why this is so, let us examine the various components of the wire-transfer systems to determine whether systemic problems could actually arise.

A bank that fails would be unlikely to have substantial daylight overdrafts on Fedwire because transactions by problem banks are monitored on a real-time basis and the Federal Reserve controls its exposure by limiting the payments it accepts from problem banks roughly to equal the payments these banks are receiving. But even if a bank's shaky condition went undetected, so that close monitoring and control of daylight overdrafts did not occur, the Federal Reserve would absorb any losses. Other banks and their customers would not be injured; there would be no systemic collapse.

Problem banks using CHIPS are also closely monitored (in real time) and their payment liabilities severely limited. If a bank were declared insolvent and prevented from settling when it owed funds on CHIPS, however, other banks in the system would be injured. Although the chances of this occurring are slim, participants in CHIPS have committed to guarantee payment through a loss-sharing arrangement that will effectively prevent the contagion from spreading. When this procedure is in place in early 1991, systemic risk on CHIPS will virtually be eliminated.

In addition to these factors, losses to either the Federal Reserve or surviving members of CHIPS would occur only if a failed bank were closed or its payments suspended before final settlement on CHIPS and Fedwire. Under existing procedures it is highly unlikely that bank failures could interfere with wire transfers. There appear to be only two possibilities. The first involves actual closure or suspension of activities of a large U.S. bank before final settlement is achieved on the wire systems. This has never happened, but it conceivably could. Such action would require the bank's primary supervisor to declare the institution insolvent *and* the FDIC to block the bank's funds payments before final settlement. The FDIC would either have to close the bank physically during the day or refuse to allow it to pay funds the bank had committed to pay. The low probability that the FDIC would take such action explains why CHIPS participants are willing to guarantee settlement finality. When it comes to U.S. banks a participating institution is unlikely to fail to settle.

The second way that bank failures could create systemic losses with CHIPS involves foreign banks. American authorities have no control over the timing of the closing of an insolvent foreign bank or over the way a closed foreign bank will deal with its obligations to pay funds owed. Experience with the failure of Germany's Herstatt bank to meet foreign exchange commitments in 1974 showed dramatically that closure of a foreign bank could leave it unable to meet payment obligations, imposing losses on U.S. banks. Should closure of a foreign bank occur before settlement, CHIPS participants would lose. A "Herstatt problem" would be unlikely to arise again because foreign banking authorities are now well aware of the international ramifications. If the problem did arise, CHIPS participants under the emerging system would have to make good on the foreign bank's net obligations, incurring losses in the process. These banks would suffer, but the cost would be spread among all participants and the payments system would not be threatened.

With existing procedures for handling large insolvent U.S. banks, systemic risk arising out of the wire-transfer system is nil; the prospect of either solvent banks or the Federal Reserve sustaining losses from funds owed on the payment wires is remote. In practice, the FDIC allows insolvent banks to fulfill their wire-transfer obligations. This is an important reason why large insolvent banks are not closed but rather continue to operate somehow until an acquisition can be arranged. As long as this policy remains in place, defaults by large U.S. banks on wire-transfer obligations cannot occur. Furthermore, it is possible to continue the policy of allowing large insolvent banks to complete their wire-transfer obligations while subjecting their uninsured depositors to loss. These depositors need not be protected in order to protect the payments system. The only risk to the payments system is that a foreign bank using CHIPS might default on net wire-transfer obligations accumulated during the day. The primary function of guaranteeing payment on CHIPS will be to eliminate the potential systemic consequences of such defaults.

Still, the Federal Reserve opts to prop up insolvent institutions until takeovers can be arranged by the FDIC. Why find out whether refusing credit to a large insolvent bank will trigger panic or threaten the payments system when the issue can be avoided altogether by making the discount window available? Unfortunately, by fighting each fire as it comes along, the Fed robs the market of whatever discipline might remain, assuring more and larger fires in the future. The Federal Reserve's approach, like the FDIC's, leads to more risk taking by banks and more frequent insolvencies, putting added strain on the insurance system.

Some Proposals for Reforming the Existing Regulatory Process

Bank regulation and the federal safety net are not working well. Congress recently eased the most pressing problems with FIRREA by increasing deposit insurance premiums to replenish the insurance funds and by correcting the worst abuses in the savings and loan industry. The regulatory agencies have begun to impose more severe capital requirements. But awareness is growing that these measures will not suffice.[17]

There is scope within the regulatory structure for further reforms by encouraging market discipline, improving the way deposit insurance is administered, and giving the regulators more power to cope with difficulties. However, revolutionary changes in the financial system have rendered the New Deal approach to regulation and the safety net ineffective; reforms based on that approach are likely to be short-lived. But the reforms discussed below would produce some improvements, at least temporarily, and perhaps more important, several of them could play a vital role in facilitating the transition to the more fundamental changes described in the next chapter.

When all depositors and creditors are protected, virtually the entire burden of containing bank risk falls on the regulators, and they are not up to this demanding task. The regulators' burden could be reduced and

17. In FIRREA, Congress recognized the need for further action; the act requires the Treasury Department to conduct a full-scale study of deposit insurance and various facets of bank regulation and to make recommendations for additional reforms.

bank risk taking controlled more effectively if large depositors (including holders of negotiable CDs and bank Eurodollar obligations) were made to bear some risk. Faced with the possibility of losing money if their banks failed, these depositors would have incentive to monitor bank performance and to discipline risky banks by shifting to less risky institutions or by insisting on interest rate premiums and larger bank capital to compensate. Thus, the actions of large uninsured and unprotected depositors, behaving in their self-interest, would exert market discipline, making it difficult and costly for banks to take on excessive risk.

Of course, many banks are prudently managed; putting some depositors and other creditors at risk would not lead to any substantive changes. But those institutions that engaged in risky ventures and those with insufficient capital would be forced by market pressures to change. Faced with the prospect of losing customers or paying substantially higher interest rates for unprotected deposits and other sources of funds, such banks would be forced to cut back on risk and to increase their capital positions to entice depositors and other creditors.

Market discipline provided by those with money at risk would reinforce rather than replace government regulation and supervision of banks; the regulators' job would become easier and more manageable. Yet adding market influence would not eliminate bank failures. Those with funds at stake would make mistakes concerning the riskiness of banks, and unforeseen events could force an otherwise solvent bank into failure. But market forces could administer powerful preventive medicine against the incidence of bank failure.

In principle, all that is needed to impose market discipline is to stop protecting depositors with balances in excess of the statutory insurance limit (currently $100,000). This is done now when a failed bank is closed and the FDIC pays off insured depositors, but we have seen that these payouts occur infrequently, usually only for small banks. But the FDIC could continue to assist takeovers while subjecting uninsured depositors to loss. This is accomplished by having the FDIC charge the cost of subsidizing a takeover against the amount that a failed bank owes its uninsured depositors and other creditors.[18] In effect, this subordinates the claims on a failed bank's assets of these depositors and creditors to the claim of the FDIC. The FDIC would lose when the value of a failed bank's assets is less than its *insured* liabilities. In this circum-

18. Because arranging a takeover could take a long time, the FDIC could charge the estimated cost, returning any overestimate that might materialize.

stance, the failed bank's uninsured deposits and other unsecured debts would be wiped out and the FDIC would still have to subsidize a takeover or absorb the cost of winding up the business of what is left. But in most instances, particularly for large banks with their sizable amounts of uninsured deposits and other debt, a failed bank's assets would exceed its insured liabilities by a sufficient margin to leave something for uninsured depositors and other creditors.

It would be too radical to move in one step from the existing situation in which uninsured depositors at large banks are totally protected to one in which they are completely at risk. A middle ground is provided by coinsurance, wherein the costs of bank failures are borne jointly by the FDIC and uninsured depositors.[19] For example, the FDIC might be responsible for 80 percent of the loss, with uninsured depositors responsible for the remaining 20 percent. Coinsurance would extend FDIC insurance to 80 percent of any deposit balance in excess of the statutory insurance limit. This would introduce market discipline for large banks without abandoning all protection for their major depositors. Coinsurance also has the advantage that it allows closures and FDIC-assisted takeovers of failed banks to be treated alike. In the case of closures, deposit balances up to the statutory insurance limit would be paid off in full, while balances above the insurance limit would be covered up to the coinsurance limit, 80 percent in our example. The same formula would be applied for FDIC-assisted takeovers, with holders of deposit balances above the insurance limit responsible for up to 20 percent of the amount of funds they have committed to a failed bank to finance the takeover cost. Coinsurance would end the discriminatory practice by which large depositors at failed banks that are closed are treated more harshly than those with funds committed to failed banks that receive FDIC takeover assistance.

Introducing coinsurance would provide much-needed market discipline while ending discrimination against small banks. The extent of coinsurance imposed on large depositors could be increased over time, providing even greater discipline. In principle, the protection provided by the FDIC to large depositors could eventually fall to zero.

Subjecting large checking account balances to coinsurance could pose problems because these balances can be shifted at a moment's notice by wire transfer, and the chances of silent runs by unprotected depositors would be particularly great. Large and rapid shifts of funds by these checking account customers could cause financial distortions

19. Coinsurance could also apply to unsecured interbank loans to failed banks.

and require Federal Reserve intervention. These problems are not as great as they might appear because wire transfers of funds from problem banks are closely monitored and controlled under both Fedwire and CHIPS. Large depositors would find it impossible to shift their funds quickly. This would limit the extent of disruptions. There is much to be said, however, for offering safe checking accounts no matter how much money is held by an individual or corporation (see chapter 5). But more fundamental reforms are required to achieve this objective.

Determining the limit for full insurance coverage is another important issue. The current limit of $100,000 is perhaps satisfactory for big banks because they have large corporate customers whose negotiable CDs and Eurodollar deposits far exceed the limit. These banks have plenty of customers to bear risk and exert restraint. The situation is different for small banks and many thrifts. Most, if not all, of their deposit accounts are for amounts at or below the insurance limit. Introducing coinsurance would put few, if any, of their customers at risk; thus, there would be little gain in market discipline for these institutions.

Market discipline can be achieved for small banks and thrifts, and increased somewhat for large institutions, by limiting the total amount of insurance available to each depositor and applying coinsurance for account balances in excess of the limit. For this to be effective, however, customers must be prevented from spreading their accounts among a number of banks and thrifts, maintaining balances in each at or below the insurance limit. Today, brokers distribute funds for customers in chunks of $100,000 or less at each institution. Computer and telecommunications technology allows this to be done inexpensively, and the costs fall steadily over time. Suppose the maximum insurance coverage were reduced to $25,000: brokers would just have to spread the money among more institutions. The cost of depositing $100,000 in one institution is less than spreading it among four, but the extra cost would not be substantial. In practice, simply reducing the insurance limit might actually bring more banks (and thrifts) into the brokered deposit network. This could even be the case for large banks that have to pay higher interest rates for large accounts subject to coinsurance. These banks would have incentive to use deposit brokers to bring in lower-cost, fully insured deposits.

A solution to this problem lies not with trying to outlaw deposit brokers but with limiting each depositor to a maximum amount of insurance protection no matter how many accounts and how many depositories are used. Each depositor would be entitled to a maximum of $100,000 insurance protection with balances in excess of that amount subject to coinsurance. Certain restrictions should be imposed, however, to make this reform meaningful. Technological advances will continue to reduce the costs of spreading accounts among more and more banks. Though it is cumbersome, and after some point impractical, to spread checking accounts, there are few practical limits for other types of accounts. Account spreading is beneficial to large depositors because it reduces the losses they sustain when any one bank fails, but it has the disadvantage of reducing their incentive to seek out safe banks. To take an extreme example, a depositor who could spread $100,000 equally among all the nation's banks would have less than $8 in each. Account spreading can be curtailed and depositor discipline encouraged by stipulating that depositors can only spread insured account balances among a limited number of banks and thrifts at any one time and that each of these institutions must be specified by depositors in advance of failure. The number of institutions is arbitrary: a maximum of five seems small enough to avoid substantial account spreading while large enough to provide depositors the convenience of using several depositories. Depositors would be free to change the institutions they select, but there could be no more than five at a time. Any depositor could have accounts in more than the five identified institutions, but all balances in those would be subject to coinsurance.

Restricting the number of institutions in which a depositor can have fully insured accounts should increase the incentive for relatively large depositors to exert discipline on their depositories. But a depositor with as much as $500,000 can spread the money equally among five preselected institutions. Should only one fail the depositor is fully protected; he or she is paid off by the FDIC and redeposits in a solvent bank that is specified for insurance or sees the funds transferred to a solvent bank that acquires the insolvent one. In either case, the depositor suffers no loss. He or she is back as before with five banks and $100,000 of insurance. This relatively large depositor has little incentive to select safe banks. Reducing the amount of insurance the depositor can receive following failure of a designated depository restores a measure of risk and impels the depositor to choose wisely. Although any specific proposal to reduce insurance coverage is necessarily arbitrary, the one that follows appears reasonable. We can think of the depositor above as having used up the $100,000 insurance quota. He or she can earn it back by avoiding failed banks in the future. Following a failure, the depositor's insurance quota is reduced by 80 percent for the next year, from $100,000 to $20,000. Should any or all of the depositor's designated banks fail during that year, only $20,000 of the account balances receive full insurance, with any excess subject to coinsurance. If no failures occur, the depositor earns another $20,000 of coverage, bringing the total to $40,000. After five years, if no failures occur at banks the depositor has designated, insurance coverage is returned to the full $100,000. Depositors with initial claims of less than $100,000 would be treated in a similar manner. For example, a $50,000 claim would reduce the insured depositor's insurance quota from $100,000 to $60,000,[20] which would return in five years to the full $100,000. This procedure would shield truly small depositors from any loss.

Market discipline could be increased further by requiring banks and thrifts to issue subordinated debt. In the event that a failed bank closes, the holders of this debt would be paid off only after both the FDIC and large depositors and other nonsubordinated creditors subject to coinsurance satisfied their claims. For assisted takeovers, the FDIC would assess its estimated costs against subordinated debt holders before collecting from general creditors and depositors subject to coinsurance.

Subordinated debt holders would bear greater risk than depositors subject to coinsurance and general creditors and would therefore have the greatest incentive to control bank risk by imposing risk premiums and withholding further credit for risky banks. In addition, subordinated debt holders would be allowed to place covenants in debt contracts providing protection against unsound behavior. For example, holders of subordinated debt could require accelerated repayment should a bank's ratio of equity to assets fall below a minimum value. The prospect of repaying a substantial amount of debt on short notice would be a powerful motivation for banks to maintain adequate capital.

To summarize, market discipline would be achieved by creating four classes of deposits and other credit. Class one, receiving total insurance coverage, comprises deposit accounts up to the insurance limit. Class two, which is subjected to coinsurance, includes all deposit account balances above the insurance limit. Class three, which has no insurance protection whatsoever, is composed of general credit extended to banks. Class four is subordinated debt. This arrangement would allow financial markets freedom to evaluate bank management and practices while placing risk on those who are best able to bear it. It must be stressed, however, that discipline can develop only if depositors and creditors lose when there is a bank failure. The crucial reform is to make

20. Fifty thousand dollars of unused quota plus $10,000 as 20 percent of $50,000 used.

large depositors and other creditors suffer if they commit funds to a bank or thrift that later collapses.

Some additional productive mileage can be wrung from the existing regulatory structure, particularly if the regulators' burden is reduced by letting the market share control. Urging regulators to exercise greater diligence and allowing them to retain larger and better-trained staffs could lead to some improvement; imposing and vigorously enforcing substantially higher capital requirements for banks (and thrifts) would contribute even more. But it is difficult to go much beyond reforms like these within the existing regulatory approach without creating new problems to replace former ones. The nature of these potential problems is revealed by reviewing some recent proposals for changing the ways that regulators go about their jobs.

A proposal offered by the Brookings Institution would go beyond increasing regulatory vigilance to require the FDIC to close a bank or arrange a takeover if its equity capital falls below some minimum percentage of total assets, perhaps 1 or 2 percent.[21] Control of the bank would pass to the FDIC when the bank's equity hit the lower limit. Establishing such a minimum threshold for action would have the benefit of allowing the FDIC to anticipate what would probably happen anyway. Typically, when a bank starts to experience massive loan losses or some other source of trouble, conditions continue to deteriorate for some time and often prove to be worse than what appears on the bank's books. If the FDIC waits until the bank is technically insolvent before taking action, the value of the bank's assets may already have fallen far below its liabilities. This has led to serious losses for the FDIC.

But early closure also penalizes banks that would not fail. In principle, this problem could be mitigated by continuing to allow a bank to operate if it is solvent (positive equity capital) but assessing assets, liabilities, and equity capital by market (economic) rather than book values. Often banks' book values bear little resemblance to the true value of their assets and liabilities: on the negative side, poorly performing loans that have not yet been written off may be carried on the books at their full par value though their true value is far less. Similarly, bonds hold book value equal to their original purchase price, and long-term, fixed-rate loans are carried at par even when a rise in interest rates has depressed their market values. On the positive side, a drop in interest rates can raise market values of bonds and fixed-rate loans above their book values. Furthermore, banks have assets such as buildings that are

21. *Blue Print for Restructuring America's Financial Institutions.*

carried on the books at their original cost less depreciation even though their current market value is far higher. The same goes for subsidiaries such as brokerage firms and ownership of foreign banks that are carried at their purchase prices rather than their true market value. The "true" amount of capital in a bank is the difference between the aggregate market value of its assets and the market value of its liabilities. This may differ significantly, in either a positive or negative direction, from what appears on the books.

The true economic values of assets and equity for a bank in trouble are often substantially less than book values. The FDIC discovers the extent to which the book values of assets exceed their true values when it closes a bank or arranges a takeover. If insolvency were based on economic values rather than book values, the FDIC could step in more quickly and limit its losses.

The market approach is feasible and accurate when valuing such assets as bonds and such liabilities as negotiable CDs that are traded in organized markets. Furthermore, with the development of secondary markets and securitization, mortgage loans, many consumer loans, and even some business loans can be valued at market. The same goes for buildings and other property. For many bank assets and liabilities, qualified appraisers are thus able to obtain objective, verifiable valuation by using market data. These assets and liabilities can be "marked to market"; that is, their book values are replaced by market values. But there are large volumes of assets for which objective market valuation is not possible. No markets exist for idiosyncratic business loans and other assets whose values depend in large part on information not readily communicated to others. Yet these are the very areas where banks provide a critical service and where they are exposed to the risk of large losses. "Market valuation" of these assets by the FDIC would have to be estimated indirectly and would be inherently subjective and arbitrary; the estimates could not be verified by an independent third party.

Even if market values could somehow be determined and agreed upon, the "going-concern" value of a bank may exceed the algebraic sum of its individual assets and liabilities. Its true total value can only be determined by seeing what someone would pay for it, but there is no practical way for the FDIC to obtain "phantom bids" on a bank on the chance it may be insolvent. The going-concern value of an institution is not a trivial issue. When the LDC debt crisis hit in the early 1980s, the nation's largest banks incurred huge economic losses because much of the credit extended LDCs was uncollectible. Had strict market accounting been used, several of these banks would have been declared insolvent, but subsequent events proved that they were able to achieve sufficient earnings from other activities to compensate for the losses and regain economic solvency. As a further example, most thrifts became insolvent on a marked-to-market basis when interest rates shot up in the early 1980s, producing huge losses in the market values of their fixed-rate mortgage loans. Yet when interest rates subsequently fell, the market values of these mortgage loans rose, returning many thrifts to solvency. It is difficult to see the benefit of using market accounting to close institutions that are viable in the longer run. But market accounting would be useful in evaluating the viability of thrifts. Many did not return to economic solvency when market interest rates fell in 1982. It would have been far cheaper to close these thrifts in 1982 rather than waiting until 1989 or later.

Market accounting is particularly difficult for banks, however. The FDIC would be given tremendous power if it were allowed to use market accounting as the sole basis for establishing insolvency. It would have incentive to protect the insurance fund by placing low values on assets without markets and using other methods to obtain low measures of equity positions, allowing it to force early closures or takeovers. It is questionable policy to allow the FDIC as beneficiary to be the arbiter of valuation. Viable as well as nonviable institutions could fall under its ax.

In spite of its deficiencies, market accounting could play a productive role in providing useful information on a bank's condition. The regulatory agencies should measure assets, liabilities, and capital in terms of market values to the extent feasible and compare these to book values and other indicators of each institution's true condition. Market valuation should be a factor, but not the only factor, in determining whether regulatory action is called for, including whether a takeover is warranted.

The massive bailout of the thrifts' insurance fund has led to growing pressure by Congress and others to protect the FDIC against virtually any loss. Evidence of this overreaction is found in FIRREA, which gives the FDIC authority to impose "cross-guarantees," requiring commonly controlled banks and thrifts to reimburse it for losses incurred in closing or assisting a takeover of an affiliated depository institution. (Depository institutions are commonly controlled if they are owned by the same holding company or if one depository institution is controlled by another.) In effect, the act allows the FDIC to shift its losses to banks and thrifts that themselves have done nothing wrong but happen to be affiliated with an institution that fails.

This provision was ill-advised, not only because it is arbitrary. More important, it undermines the principle of corporate separateness, which is essential for achieving long-lasting reform. Arbitrariness arises not only because it is left to the FDIC to determine whether to impose cross-guarantees but also because the FDIC's ability to impose them depends upon whether a failed bank (or thrift) happens to be affiliated with other insured depository institutions. If a bank has no affiliates, the FDIC has no deep pockets to reach into and must sustain the loss. For purposes of protecting the FDIC's fund, banks in a multibank holding company are treated effectively as branches rather than separate corporate entities, even though they are not accorded advantages that come from being branches. These banks—along with all others—have contributed to the insurance fund, but only they can be required to guarantee the fund against losses. It is difficult to find any justification for this policy except as a method for limiting payouts from the insurance fund.

Cross-guarantees might succeed in limiting each bank's risk, but more likely they would simply discourage the operation of multibank holding companies. Banks can avoid the burden of providing cross-guarantees by ending their affiliation with a holding company. In addition, cross-guarantees confound market discipline for institutions in a multibank holding company. Large depositors and other creditors would bear the risk of all depository institutions in a holding company but would only be able to discipline the activities of the one to which they provided funds. This situation would encourage those at risk to provide funds only to banks and thrifts that lack affiliates, putting multibank holding companies in an untenable position.

FIRREA allows the FDIC to impose cross-guarantees only on insured and affiliated depository institutions, but it would be a small additional step to require parent holding companies to compensate the FDIC for its losses should an affiliated depository fail. A congressional committee has proposed that this step be taken.[22] This would certainly reduce the exposure of the FDIC's fund—at the cost of substantial distortions. Furthermore, granting the FDIC a potential claim on their resources, parent companies, and indirectly nondepository affiliates, would find it difficult if not impossible to raise funds because of the risk to their creditors. The principal of corporate separateness that otherwise protects these creditors would be undermined.

22. U.S. House of Representatives, Committee on Government Operations, "Modernization of the Financial Services Industry."

Forcing early closures or takeovers of weak but solvent banks and drawing on the resources of affiliated institutions could greatly reduce payouts from the insurance fund. But to go this route would severely damage viable banks and banking efficacy generally. Banks perform an important economic function by taking on risk. They should earn the rewards of this service and bear the consequence of failure when they do a poor job. The insurance fund has been accumulated by assessments on banks, and it exists to defray the losses from failure; payouts should occur. It would be a perversion of deposit insurance to pursue policies to assure that the insurance fund would not have to be used.

The art in administering deposit insurance, given the current regulatory environment, is to balance the level of assessments and the size of the fund against the amount of risks that banks face. Bank risk is constrained by regulation, but every bank pays the FDIC the same insurance assessment regardless of its soundness. This tends to encourage risk taking, leading to greater burdens on the regulatory process and greater assessments on all banks, risky and less risky alike.

This problem has led to proposals for deposit insurance that would peg assessments to risk, creating an incentive for banks to behave in a prudent manner.[23] Risk-based insurance assessments could in principle replace much of the current regulatory discipline, but they would probably supplement existing procedures. Under existing arrangements, banks have a flat insurance assessment but are subject to a wide array of regulatory restrictions designed to control their risk. If a bank is judged to be behaving in too risky a manner, it is criticized by its supervisors. If this proves ineffective, the regulators can use harsher methods, including cease-and-desist orders. Risk-based insurance would supplement these regulatory restrictions with economic incentives. A bank would be told to cut back on its risk, and insurance premiums would be raised until it did.

Major practical problems hinder implementation of risk-based deposit insurance. The root of the problem is that regulators are not very good at anticipating difficulties, and nothing in risk-based insurance *per se* would change this situation. In practice, it is difficult for them to determine the risks that banks are taking. Years later, it is easy to say that in the 1970s certain banks should not have concentrated so much of their loans in agriculture, energy, or Latin America. But these issues were much less clear at the time the loans were made. And what about all the risks that do not show up on the balance sheet, such as loan

23. See, e.g., Kane, *Gathering Crisis in Federal Deposit Insurance.*

commitments and guarantees, daylight overdrafts to corporate customers, and the like? Would banking regulators anticipate problems before they occur and set insurance premiums accordingly?

Establishing risk-based insurance ascribes to the regulators an ability to identify and measure risk that they do not possess. During the 1970s, when large banks ran up their leverage and amassed huge amounts of loans to LDCs, the regulators apparently did not see the risk. Most banks were doing well during this period, so it was difficult for the regulators to find fault. Risk-based insurance would not change this situation.

Beyond that, it is difficult to determine reasonable assessment schedules. The relevant concept of risk is for the whole banking firm, not just for a part of its asset portfolio or a particular off-balance-sheet activity. Individual risks cannot be added together in any simple way, and there are no agreed-upon or infallible methods for measuring a bank's aggregate amount of risk. The complex and arbitrary risk-based capital standards recently imposed on banks do not lead to optimism about the FDIC's ability to develop effective risk-based insurance assessments.

The best way to view risk-based insurance is as a tax imposed against risky banks; it is inappropriate to think in terms of actuarially fair insurance. The amount of loss that a risky bank might inflict on the FDIC depends critically upon the circumstances and upon how the regulators respond. If a failing bank is in a prime location or has some other attractive feature, it will attract buyers and put only a small claim on the fund. If it is less attractive, it will absorb more of the fund. Should premiums be based on this consideration as well? If so, it might turn out that some banks could pursue risk if they were candidates for takeover but not otherwise. Neither is the degree of risk that banks face independent of the macroeconomic policies the government pursues. If policy produces a tranquil economic and financial environment, bank risk is lower than if policy contributes to instability. Blame for much of the high inflation of the 1970s and the huge recession of the early 1980s, generated by a credit squeeze to eliminate inflation, can be laid on the government's doorstep, yet risk-based insurance would allow the government to pursue policies that increase bank risk, then turn around and decree higher insurance assessments because risk has increased.

Finally, risk-based insurance gives the regulators arbitrary power. Banks engaging in activities the regulators do not like may be hit with higher assessments even if risk has not actually risen. Virtually any new activity would probably be labeled risky; regulators instinctively dislike new activities because they do not understand them.[24] More generally, risk-based insurance gives regulators the ability to punish banks they do not like and to reward banks they do. In the absence of objective standards this degree of discretion is dangerous.

Pegging insurance assessments to a bank's past performance could remedy these practical problems. If a bank suffers large losses from any source, be it bad loans, poor management, off-balance-sheet risk, or whatever, its insurance assessments will rise. If a bank knows that it will be penalized, it will be inhibited from taking risks to begin with. This approach dispenses with the need to anticipate potential problems; it simply looks at performance. But such an approach could also exacerbate a bank's problems and even force it into bankruptcy. If a bank has a string of bad luck, it will suffer losses that weaken its condition. Should the FDIC penalize the bank by raising its insurance assessments, the bank becomes even weaker and its chances of failure rise.[25] Before banks get into trouble, the FDIC's threat of higher assessments might discourage them from taking on so much risk, but if unfavorable events get them into difficulties anyway, higher assessments could trigger failures.[26] If the FDIC does not raise assessments, however, banks will learn that running risks and sustaining losses will not result in new costs. The threat of higher assessments turns out to be empty, and insurance assessments based on actual performance cannot work.

Risk-based insurance could be effective only if sufficiently large assessments were imposed on risky activities to discourage banks from engaging in them in the first place. But this requires an ability to identify risky activities and monitor bank performance that regulators do not possess. One must conclude that risk-based insurance simply cannot perform an effective service. Far better to rely on market discipline exerted by large depositors and other creditors whose funds are at risk. The risk premiums and capital standards they impose would be more effective than risk-based insurance assessments imposed by the FDIC.

24. For example, regulators resisted allowing banks to engage in transactions in interest rate futures markets on the grounds that they involved speculation, whereas many banks were using the markets to reduce risk.
25. Automobile insurers would not raise their rates for drivers who get speeding tickets if this would increase the chance that these drivers would get into a wreck.
26. This was the quandary faced by the FSLIC when it raised assessments in an effort to cover its massive losses, and it limited Congress's ability to raise assessments to generate revenue for the Savings Association Insurance Fund established under FIRREA.

Implementation of proposals to close banks before outright insolvency or to draw on the resources of holding company affiliates or to introduce risk-based deposit insurance would probably cause more problems than they would solve. It would be effective, however, to revamp the approach to regulating bank holding companies. As we have seen, these holding companies are regulated much as banks are, with their own capital requirements and supervision enforced by the Federal Reserve Board. This approach compels the Fed to oversee an ever-widening set of activities and institutions as bank holding companies are allowed additional powers. Attention is distracted from overseeing banks to supervising nonbank components of holding companies, resulting in poorer regulation. In addition, regulation of nonbank elements of bank holding companies, such as finance companies, securities companies, and mortgage banking affiliates, makes it difficult for these to compete with companies not affiliated with holding companies but providing the same services. The competitive disadvantage would be particularly great if parent companies, and indirectly nonbank affiliates, were required to compensate the FDIC for losses should failures occur. Faced with this prospect, bank holding companies would have incentive to shift activities from their nonbank affiliates to their banks to take advantage of the federal safety net. The activities performed by banks could expand substantially, requiring greater regulatory effort to control risk.

These problems could be avoided by separating banks from other elements of their holding companies and regulating only banks. At the same time, the Federal Reserve would be given greater authority to protect banks from the misfortunes of nonbank elements of their holding companies by further limiting transactions between banks and other holding company constituents and by including daylight overdrafts in credit ceilings. With tighter controls and harsh penalties, including criminal sentences, it is exceedingly unlikely that a bank could be injured by its holding company. The next step is to abandon the largely vain hope that bank holding companies can be used to help defray the FDIC's costs of handling failures. We have seen that efforts to exploit bank holding companies in this way would be largely self-defeating as well as inefficient. With banks effectively insulated from the fortunes of their holding companies, there would be no need to subject parent companies and nonbank affiliates to banking regulation. This would leave them free to raise funds—completely uninsured and unprotected by the government—in order to compete in the marketplace and engage in new activities. The reform would have the singular advantage of allowing the banking regulators to focus on regulating banks while not inhibiting financial innovation because new activities that are deemed too risky for banks would be conducted by nonbanking elements of bank holding companies.

For reasons elaborated in this chapter, there is scope for patching up the existing regulatory environment by encouraging greater market discipline while strengthening and streamlining regulation. These improvements will likely be short-lived, however, because economic forces contributing to financial integration will continue to erode the niche carved out for banking by the New Deal reforms, making it tougher for banks to compete as position takers, issuing deposit liabilities and holding loans. Banks will continue to experience difficulties because they will have progressively less of economic value to offer. We have seen that money market and other mutual funds provide the equivalent of depository services, while much of the loan business of depositories has been taken over by commercial paper, the bond market, and mortgage bankers. Many of the historically important areas of lending are becoming securitized, including consumer credit. In light of these developments, it will prove increasingly difficult for banks to remain profitable while at the same time providing the degree of safety required for successful operation of the federal safety net.

A whole new approach to banking and financial regulation is needed that takes the profound implications of financial integration into account. The final chapter is devoted to developing and defending a proposal to radically restructure the way in which banks are organized, operated, and controlled.

5

A New Approach

The current regulatory approach has outlived its usefulness. Without fundamental changes, banking's problems are likely to worsen as financial markets become ever more integrated. A new approach that recognizes and takes advantage of the inevitable consequences of integration in the creation and delivery of financial services is the best solution. Banking must lose its highly regulated and protected status, but at the same time it is crucial to protect the safety and soundness of the nation's monetary and payments systems.

Disaster is hardly imminent; the nation is not hovering on the brink of financial collapse. But maintaining the *status quo* invites risky actions, wastes resources, distorts incentives, interferes with monetary policy, and only postpones the thoroughgoing regulatory changes that eventually will have to occur. Taxpayers will be shouldering the immense cost of the S&L crisis for many years to come. It is imperative that banking be reformed so as to avert a future crisis that could be much more costly.

The considerable increase in bank failures and the spectacular bailouts of a few giant banks and much of the thrift industry have received a good deal of media attention. But these are merely symptoms of the more fundamental problem: financial integration has destroyed many of the unique characteristics of depository institutions, but forced

127

specialization and government protection have made it impossible for them to evolve into enterprises compatible with the new environment. Because of government protection, depositories have overexpanded their deposits and lending, with the consequence that profits are low and risks are high. And forced specialization inhibits depositories from shifting from deposit taking and lending into other, more profitable financial activities.

The key to solving the problem does not lie with tightening the intensity and scope of bank regulation, which would lead only to more banking activities being conducted outside of conventional banks. It is simply impossible to regulate everyone. Because of market integration and technological advances, monetary and financial activities are fungible, and regulation cannot block services from being performed. It can only affect who provides them.

All attempts at regulation are not futile and undesirable. The approach described here may seem radical, but that is because the New Deal approach to bank regulation is so radically at odds with what is appropriate for the future. Because we need fundamental changes, rather than frantic attempts to solve crises, it is desirable to step back, question how banking and financial services should be structured to best meet the needs of business and society, and then address these issues.

The key to finding a solution to the regulatory problem lies in asking a simple but infrequently posed question. What are the objectives? They are to achieve a safe and efficient monetary system, and stable and reliable sources of credit, while avoiding undue risk taking, financial instability, and exposure to future government bailouts. But to address these objectives most productively it is necessary to extend our thinking beyond the specific kinds of firms that happen to provide various financial services at the present time. Who offers which financial services is the consequence of the current regulatory structure. If meaningful progress is to be made in analyzing the objectives of regulation, it is necessary to stop thinking in terms of specific types of institutions and to start thinking in terms of types of financial *functions.* It is the functions that are at issue, not who happens to perform them. This proposition is important both for the monetary system and for sources of credit.

That the nation's monetary system—mediums of exchange (money) and the payments system—be safe and efficient is paramount. In the United States, as in other industrialized countries, the monetary system is operated largely by the private sector, subject to government regulation. Among the mediums of exchange only currency and coins are liabilities of the government and hence always free from default risk.[1] Other mediums, such as checking account balances at banks and thrifts, are the liabilities of private businesses to repay on demand and are not completely safe. Deposit insurance has made this form of money safe for relatively small depositors, but uninsured checking account balances are safe only to the extent that FDIC-assisted takeovers and other methods provide *de facto* protection.

The payments system is likewise a mixture of governmental and private efforts. The part of the payments system using the Federal Reserve's check collection and electronic funds transfer services is safe because the Fed guarantees its obligations. If a bank from which payments originate defaults, the Federal Reserve will make good on the transactions. Much of the payments system works outside the Federal Reserve, however. Checks are cleared through private clearinghouses, and EFTs among banks occur via private systems. Here default of a bank from which payments originate can cause losses for other private parties including banks. This risk is reduced but not eliminated by regulatory restrictions and private risk-sharing arrangements.

It makes little sense for some users of money and the payments system to be safe while others are not. A crucial objective of any regulatory revamping should be to offer everyone a safe monetary system.

A safe monetary system is needed to achieve the macroeconomic objective of economic stability, but there is another objective. The public desires a safe haven in an asset whose value is immune to uncertain market forces. This is the primary reason that deposit insurance is so popular; people know that their money is safe. Deposit insurance guarantees that the asset (a checking account balance) can be redeemed at par.[2]

Most people are probably not even aware that the "real" reason for deposit insurance is macroeconomic: to improve the stability of the monetary system. They simply view it as providing a safe haven. This may appear to be splitting hairs. After all, the reason deposit insurance

1. Currency and coin are not, of course, immune to erosion of purchasing power caused by inflation.

2. Securities issued by the U.S. Treasury have no default risk; holders are guaranteed interest payments and repayment of principal at maturity. The values of outstanding government securities fluctuate with market conditions, however. They are not repayable on demand at par and are not risk-free. But short-term government securities experience relatively small price fluctuations and are close to being a risk-free asset. Large minimum denominations prevent many people from holding these securities.

protects the monetary system is precisely that people know their money is safe and do not make panicked withdrawals. Although the objectives of a safe monetary system and a safe asset for the public are related, they are not identical.

The application of insurance to all kinds of accounts at banks and thrifts extended safety far beyond what is necessary for monetary stability. The holder of a five-year time account or even an IRA (individual retirement account) receives the same protection as a holder of a checking account, even though these long-term accounts pose no threat to the monetary system through bank runs. Insurance covers the spectrum of safe assets differing in maturity and interest return. On the flip side, large depositors, including businesses, are not guaranteed the safety of their checking accounts because their balances often far exceed the $100,000 insurance limit. It is appropriate to protect the safety of money and payments for users of all sizes, but protecting the monetary function does not require that nonmonetary accounts be protected as well.

It is also important to note that the availability of insurance and the provision of payments services are restricted to conventional depository institutions. This was harmless in 1933 because only depositories offered monetary services. Today, however, the situation is very different. Hundreds of billions of dollars are on deposit at money market funds, which are cut off from the benefits of federal deposit insurance and denied direct access to the payments system.

There is little economic sense in singling out banks and thrifts for special treatment. The important consideration is to provide insurance for monetary services no matter what kind of business happens to offer them. Among other benefits of this approach, it is possible to provide insurance for certain kinds of liabilities offered by various businesses without insuring all of their liabilities.

Any proposal for reforming bank regulation should be concerned with assuring that borrowers have stable, reliable sources of credit. This objective was firmly intertwined with trying to assure stability of the banking system because banks were such an important source of business loans. The banking devastation of the early 1930s involved the collapse not only of the nation's monetary system but also of the availability of credit to businesses. Because bank credit was funded largely by accounts payable on demand, the objectives of stability of money and of credit came to the same thing.

Today, monetary and credit functions are less entwined. Most of bank credit is funded not by monetary liabilities but by time accounts and other nonmonetary liabilities, and much business borrowing is conducted outside banks, using commercial paper and bond markets and other sources of credit. In principle, at least, these two objectives are now separable: assuring monetary stability does not necessarily lead to stability of credit, and stability of credit does not necessarily imply monetary stability. With the monetary and credit functions at least partially independent, the issue of credit stability must be addressed directly.

The Proposal in Outline

The proposal for banking reform that follows is designed to meet the monetary and credit objectives that have been enumerated while positioning providers of financial services to meet the needs of the twenty-first century. I shall first present it without any explanation of how to get from here to there. Once the proposal is set forth and defended as a long-term objective, I shall shift to issues of transition. There turns out to be a fairly simple means of adapting several of the proposals reviewed at the end of chapter 4 to convert gradually to the new regulatory order.

The proposed long-run approach contains two parts, presented first in outline form, then in a detailed discussion assessing each in terms of the stated objectives. Stated in the most general terms, the proposal involves abandoning the institution-specific approach of the current regulatory structure in favor of one that focuses directly on monetary and financial functions. Banks as they are known today continue to exist, as one type of business providing these functions, but banking's internal structure is changed fundamentally in a manner that protects banks' monetary activities while subjecting all their other activities to the rigors of market discipline. This is accomplished by isolating monetary activities from all others within banks. Such an isolation allows banks to offer a much wider range of activities than is currently permitted.

Monetary Service Companies

It is not necessary to assure the safety and soundness of all the activities in which banks and thrifts engage in order to protect their monetary functions. The idea here is to isolate, insure, and protect *monetary* functions while eliminating insurance and protection for all other functions. Monetary services are provided in legally separate monetary service companies (MSCs) operated within banks. These highly regulated, separately capitalized companies offer federally in-sured accounts payable on demand at par—in the form of either cur-rency or orders to pay a third party. In short, they provide the checking accounts and wire transfers currently offered by banks and thrifts. MSCs are permitted to pay interest on all their accounts, both household and business, with interest rates determined by competition among them and by their asset holdings.

Monetary service companies are highly restricted concerning the assets that they can hold. MSCs are limited to purchases of the same sorts of short-term, highly marketable, and highly rated instruments that are in the portfolios of today's money market mutual funds. These include short-term Treasury securities, highly rated commercial paper, and similar instruments. Unlike money market funds, the MSCs have a capital base and enjoy federal insurance for *all* their liabilities without limit.

Monetary service companies also provide payment services, includ-ing check clearing and electronic funds transfer. These activities have federal insurance to protect the public and other MSCs against failure of any MSC.

Rules of operation and standards of licensing for MSCs are established and enforced by the Federal Reserve, which is also authorized to super-vise these institutions and to approve mergers and acquisitions in which they are involved. The Federal Reserve also administers the federal insurance program for MSCs. Entry into the monetary services business is open to all who meet the minimum standards. Thus, banks operate their checking account and payment services business through sepa-rately capitalized MSCs. Similarly, money market mutual funds can con-vert to stock form and operate as MSCs. Furthermore, any collection of individuals or any corporate entity can operate a separately capitalized MSC, provided they meet the licensing and operating standards.

Crucial to establishing and operating an MSC is the explicit and ironclad restriction that it not lend to its owners. An MSC can provide checking accounts and payment services to its owners on the same basis as for other customers, but that is all. Thus, an MSC may be owned and operated by a bank, pay dividends, and receive capital injections, but the MSC cannot lend money to the bank, buy such market obligations as CDs, or in any other way be involved in providing funds to the bank. The same restrictions, backed by stiff criminal and civil penalties for willful violation, apply to transactions with any other owner, be it a bank holding company, securities firm, insurance company, retailer, manufacturer, private individual, or whatever. These restrictions eliminate conflicts of interest and help maintain effective corporate separateness that protects MSCs against failure of their owners.

To guarantee separation and therefore ensure that the fortunes of their owners and affiliates will not impinge on the fortunes of MSCs, legislation establishes that no MSC is responsible for the debts of related entities. For example, if an MSC is part of a bank holding company, the creditors of the parent company or its nonmonetary affiliates will have no claim on the MSC. The same restrictions hold if the MSC is part of some other financial conglomerate. Failure of any other entity cannot threaten the monetary service company. This approach is similar to how regulations in many states protect insurance companies against attacks by creditors of companies affiliated with the insurance companies in a financial conglomerate. Federal laws are to provide ironclad protection for MSCs.

With separateness established, a monetary service company is free to operate offices wherever it chooses. A banking organization, retailer, or other corporation can run an MSC in the same location as it offers other services. Further, a monetary service company is free to share personnel, information, data processing, and expertise with its affiliates so that synergies and efficiencies can be exploited. However, to protect an MSC from being operated as a "loss leader" by its owners or affiliates to attract customers to other products, the Federal Reserve is empowered to close a monetary service company if it makes chronic losses. The Fed is also authorized to set minimum capital standards for MSCs and to limit their dividend payments when such action is required to meet these standards.

Along with its supervisory functions, the Federal Reserve is authorized to impose reserve requirements on the liabilities of MSCs, just as it currently imposes reserve requirements on checking accounts of banks and thrifts. The Fed is also required to make the discount window available to MSCs and to allow them access to its check clearing and EFT systems. In effect, the Federal Reserve's current special relationship with banks and thrifts is transferred to monetary service companies. Its ability to conduct monetary policy is not weakened in any way.

Nothing in the proposal prevents a business from operating an uninsured money market fund or other institution that allows customers to withdraw their money by check or wire transfer. The object is not to make all checkable assets safe but rather to offer the public a completely safe alternative.

Financial Service Companies

The second part of the proposal is to allow all activities other than those of monetary service companies to be conducted without the regulation and supervision imposed on today's banks. The Office of the Comptroller of the Currency and the Office of Thrift Supervision disappear, as do the regulatory functions of the Federal Reserve and the FDIC relating to activities outside monetary service companies. Federal statutes and regulations concerning bank holding companies are also eliminated.

It is convenient to think of the providers of nonmonetary financial services as financial service companies (FSCs), operating in tandem with MSCs within a bank or financial conglomerate, but the actual corporate structures are left up to the owners, be they insurance companies, retailers, banks, whatever. Perhaps the easiest way to appreciate what financial service companies can do is to start with conventional banking organizations. They operate their checking account and payment services through MSCs. What remains is the nucleus of financial service companies that operate alongside MSCs. Banks' savings and time accounts, plus their other liabilities, are the obligations of FSCs.[3] Banks' lending to business and consumers and all of their other existing financial services are executed by FSCs. To this nucleus is added the ability to offer all kinds of insurance, as well as full securities underwriting, brokerage, and mutual funds, along with any other financial service that financial service companies choose. Thus, FSCs are able to provide a complete range of financial services, except for insured monetary services. An FSC can own an MSC; they can share facilities, personnel, and information; they can even operate side by side in the same offices; but the MSC is insulated from the fortunes of its owners. Bank holding companies as such disappear and are replaced by the corporate umbrellas containing MSCs and FSCs.

Financial service companies have been described by viewing them as banking organizations legally, but not physically, separated from their monetary functions and augmented by other financial activities. But we could have started with an insurance company or securities firm. In effect, FSCs are financial conglomerates. The nonmonetary part of banks and thrifts is joined with insurance, securities, mutual funds, and other financial activities.

Financial service companies are regulated in the same way that non-bank providers of financial services are currently regulated. Federal

3. Thus, about 40 percent of current banking goes to MSCs and 60 percent to FSCs.

laws concerning antitrust, securities regulation, and truth in lending apply to FSCs, as do state laws, including those that regulate insurance companies. The massive and cumbersome regulatory apparatus that currently governs banks and bank holding companies is eliminated for FSCs. No special restrictions are imposed on the transactions that can occur among components of financial service companies, but, as noted earlier, severe restrictions are placed on transactions between FSCs and their affiliated monetary service companies.

So much regulation can be eliminated primarily because none of the liabilities issued by FSCs are insured; there is no federal guarantee or protection against failure. The government is taken out of the business of protecting holders of nonmonetary liabilities issued by what are now banks and thrifts, and it is not responsible for the safety and soundness of FSCs.

Financial service companies are to have access to the Federal Reserve's discount window on an emergency basis in order to allow them to honor credit lines and to handle problems in rolling over their liabilities in the event of a severe loss of liquidity. This allows the central bank to exercise its powers as lender of last resort when a clear emergency is involved. But the discount window is not available to bail out insolvent institutions.

Although the structure of banking is fundamentally altered from a legal and regulatory perspective, it is important to appreciate that the division of functions between monetary and all other financial services is not intrusive to the public. Institutions called banks can continue to operate, providing the services they currently offer plus many more. These new banks will look much the same to the general public as their current banks. Deposits and withdrawals can be made for a variety of accounts; loans and other financial services are available. Checking accounts function the same way as they do now. The differences are that business checking accounts earn interest, there is no upper limit for insured balances, and the accounts are the liabilities of banks' monetary service companies, which can invest only in short-term marketable instruments. Customers can make deposits into time accounts, purchase mutual funds, and acquire other assets in the same offices—even use the same teller, human or electronic, for MSC and FSC business if convenient. Funds placed with banks' financial service companies, however, are at risk, and customers must be clearly informed that this is the case. Banks can use the same offices to provide credit, ranging from car and mortgage loans to various kinds of loans to business. This credit is funded not by insured checking accounts, however, but by time accounts and other liabilities issued by banks' financial service companies.

Nothing in the proposal requires institutions offering these various services to be called banks. They can call themselves whatever they want and provide whatever combination of services they find attractive. The sole restriction is that if an institution wants to offer insured checking accounts and use the Federal Reserve's funds transfer system it must do so through a separate, regulated monetary service company.

The Proposal in Detail

The proposal is such a dramatic departure from the existing regulatory approach that it is sure to produce strong criticisms concerning both its practicality and desirability. Criticisms are met most directly by testing the proposal against the established objectives. The details of the proposal will be developed in the process of seeing how well it meets these objectives.

Safety and Stability of the Monetary System

The proposal enhances the stability of the monetary system by improving the safety of both checking accounts and the payments system. Currently, accounts at banks and thrifts, which are payable on demand, are used to fund illiquid, relatively long-term, and risky loans. In the absence of heavy government intervention, the severe mismatch between the character of liabilities and assets would make checking accounts unsafe and the banking system potentially unstable. Regulation and supervision, deposit insurance, and access to the Fed's discount window are invoked to make the situation viable. Furthermore, large depositors are not covered completely by deposit insurance. Their money is at risk, a problem that has been addressed by bailing out banks, prompting the current difficulties the insurance funds and regulatory agencies face.

Money market mutual funds have demonstrated that it is possible to provide monetary services on terms attractive to the public while extending forms of credit that are highly liquid and low-risk. The assets held by the money market funds are much more compatible with their obligations than those of banks and thrifts. When it comes to provision of monetary services, the model offered by money market funds is much more attractive than the one supplied by banks. Far better to use demand obligations to purchase highly liquid and low-risk commercial paper than to finance loans to LDCs, oil drillers, commercial real estate developers, and takeover artists engaged in leveraged buyouts.

The proposed monetary service companies take money market funds one step further with a corporate structure that allows demand obligations to be offered payable at par. They also go beyond money market funds by making payment services an integral part of their activities. Monetary service companies can invest only in highly liquid, short-term, and low-risk assets traded in the money market. These include Treasury bills and notes, highly rated commercial and finance company paper, and similar instruments. With a much closer match between the character of liabilities and assets, the risk that a MSC cannot meet its demand obligations at par is vastly lower than for banks and thrifts today.

The idea is not to eliminate the risk that a monetary service company might become insolvent—to do so would prevent it from extending credit to the private sector—but rather to make the risk low enough that any insolvencies can be handled easily by deposit insurance. Three sources of risk can reduce the value of an MSC's assets below its liabilities: a large decline in the market value of its assets, defaults on the credit instruments it holds, and fraudulent activities of its employees. Risk of insolvency for MSCs is limited by requiring them to have minimum equity capital, by restricting the kinds of assets they hold while enforcing diversification standards, and by policing against fraud. Should insolvencies occur, however, federal deposit insurance protects depositors against loss. Although deposit insurance makes it highly unlikely that depositors would lose confidence in MSCs, in the event of a run on deposits the Federal Reserve would provide the resources necessary, through the discount window and open-market purchases of securities, to stabilize the situation.

Though operation of the federal safety net is similar to current arrangements for protecting accounts at banks and thrifts, the amount of regulation and oversight required for MSCs is vastly less. All the Federal Reserve needs to do is draw up a list of securities that are eligible for the portfolios of MSCs and set minimum standards for diversification. Current SEC regulations for money market funds serve as an excellent model. Supervision is reduced to determining that guidelines are followed and policing fraud.

Another fundamental difference from current practice is the complete separation of MSCs' financial operations from those of their owners, which eliminates the risk that failure of an affiliated firm could bring down a monetary service company. The possibility of such contamination under current arrangements causes the Federal Reserve much concern, leading it to regulate bank holding companies and their nonbank affiliates in an effort to protect affiliated banks. An MSC is prohibited from buying debt instruments issued by any company affiliated with it or from extending it any other forms of credit. Dividend payments are allowed, but the Federal Reserve has the authority to limit them if necessary to protect the MSC. With these legal restrictions, enforced by the Fed and backed up by severe penalties for any party that violates them, there is no reason to regulate or supervise firms that own or are affiliated with an MSC in order to protect it. This results in huge savings to the federal government.

It is difficult to overstate the importance of corporate separateness for protecting monetary service corporations. If an MSC could borrow from or lend to its parent company or affiliates, if its earnings could be stripped by these entities, and if only a veil separated it from them, then its affairs would be inexorably mingled with their fate. An MSC would be as risky as its parent or affiliate. But the severe restrictions imposed on MSCs in their dealings with affiliated FSCs erect an effective firewall separating and protecting them from losses suffered by these FSCs. Pursuit of risky activities by the unprotected financial services part of a bank will not injure its insured monetary service company.

Because the risk of failure of an MSC is small, insurance premiums can be much lower than at present. How low should the risks go? If monetary service companies were limited to holding short-term Treasury securities, they would not confront any default risk on the assets they hold. That approach has been suggested by Robert Litan and other proponents of "narrow banks."[4] It would accomplish less than one might think because these narrow banks would still have to contend with the possibility of decline in the market values of their assets caused by increases in interest rates and with the danger of fraud.

Restricting MSCs to purchasing government securities may not appear to be much of a change from what is proposed here, but the difference is fundamental. Litan and others would eliminate insured checking accounts as sources of credit to the private sector. Requiring that insured checking account balances be invested only in Treasury securities would lead to an enormous decline in the amount of funds available to private borrowers. This is neither desirable nor necessary.

4. See Litan, *What Should Banks Do?* chapter 5, and the list of references to similar proposals he provides on p. 166.

Under the arrangement proposed here, funds can flow from checking accounts at MSCs to private borrowers both directly and indirectly through unaffiliated FSCs, providing a needed source of credit, but in the form of diversified portfolios of highly liquid and low-risk market securities. In principle, as short-term loans to consumers and businesses become securitized, even these instruments would qualify.

The activities of MSCs are sufficiently circumscribed and their regulation is so straightforward that it is not necessary to rely upon large depositors for discipline; the distinction between small and large depositors can thus be eliminated. Furthermore, because MSCs hold marketable securities, their assets can easily be marked to market for purposes of assessing capital adequacy. Finally, it is feasible to assess MSCs with risk-based insurance premiums. A company that holds a large proportion of its assets in Treasury securities would have a lower premium than one that holds a lot of private securities.

It might be argued that the risks for MSCs are sufficiently low that private insurers rather than the government could provide coverage. This begs the question of systemic risk. If depositors feared that private insurers could not cover their obligations there could be runs on a number of MSCs, which, in the absence of Federal Reserve intervention, would cause a collapse in prices of the securities MSCs hold as they rush to sell them off. True, the Fed would provide assistance through the discount window and open-market operations. But such an emergency could be avoided altogether by retaining government insurance.

The government guarantees that account balances at MSCs are always payable on demand at par. All accounts at MSCs receive federal insurance; there are no restrictions as to size of the account or the type of customer—household, business, or government. But the liabilities issued by financial service companies or any other firm are not insured or guaranteed in any way. This represents a substantial reduction in the number of safe assets available to the public. Today all the savings and time accounts offered by banks and thrifts as well as their checking accounts are insured to $100,000, and larger accounts are usually protected as well. This blanket extension of insurance and guarantees to virtually all types of liabilities of banks and thrifts is what has required so much heavy-handed and ineffective regulation.

The cost to the public of limiting insurance to MSC checking accounts is the restriction in selection of safe assets. The benefit is reduced regulation, enhanced monetary stability, and elimination of taxpayer bailouts of bankrupt insurance funds. It is a relatively easy matter to back accounts payable on demand at par by the highly liquid, low-risk assets held by MSCs. But it is difficult and costly to offer an extensive array of accounts across a wide range of maturities, payable at maturity at par but backed by risky assets. Attempts to insure such an array of accounts have led to today's problems with insurance and regulation. It seems far better to insure only what is relatively easy to insure and leave other accounts at risk.

Anyone who wants a safe asset can hold an account in a MSC.[5] If the return on the asset is not all that a person wants, scores of other assets are available with varying amounts of risk. Small savers who are unable or unwilling to assess this risk scientifically might stick to accounts in MSCs, but this would not be necessary. Mutual funds of government securities and other extremely low-risk alternatives would flourish in an environment where banks and thrifts are not offering government-insured time accounts. For savers in general, various mutual funds, individual stocks and bonds, and liabilities offered by financial service companies and others are all available. Everyone is free to hold any desired combination of assets, anchored by risk-free accounts at MSCs.

It is important to realize that whereas the checking accounts offered by MSCs are totally insured, nothing prevents some other type of financial firm from offering checkable "accounts" that are uninsured. It is neither necessary nor desirable to make all checkable assets safe. Right now there are many types of assets available to the public that are payable on demand by check or wire transfers. For example, many kinds of mutual funds, including money market, stock, and bond funds, allow customers to withdraw part or all of their investment by check. The value of a customer's investment fluctuates with market conditions, however, and there is no promise to repay at par. The availability of checkable assets has increased markedly in recent years, and it is even possible for homeowners to establish a line of credit based on the equity in their houses, activating the line by writing checks. This in effect converts a highly illiquid asset into a liquid one. With the development of better technology, an increasing number of assets will become perfectly liquid in the sense that they can be either sold or borrowed against by writing a check or making a computer entry. The basic difference between these assets and the checking accounts at MSCs is that there is no government guarantee of payment at par.

With a large and growing share of the public's assets in highly liquid (checkable) but risky forms, it is possible that swings in public confi-

5. Short-term government securities are also available to those who can afford the minimum denominations.

dence concerning the safety of these assets could produce monetary and financial instability. There could be times when the public loses faith in these assets, making large and rapid shifts into accounts at MSCs, followed by optimistic times when the shifts go in the opposite direction. These actions could cause serious fluctuations in asset values. With the ability to liquidate mutual fund shares on demand, for example, a loss of public confidence could trigger massive sales of stocks and bonds in the funds. Panic could ensue if the mutual funds could not honor all the checks written against them as the value of the assets in the funds fell below the value of the checks written. This would give holders of mutual fund shares the incentive to be first in line with a check in the hope of collecting before capital values plummet. Furthermore, those who successfully withdrew from mutual funds would place the money in MSCs. These institutions would swell in size, forcing up the prices of Treasury bills, commercial paper, and other securities and reducing their rate of return, thereby adding to the distortions.

It is easy to get carried away with horror stories like these. The ability to use checks to switch between mutual funds and other investments on the one hand and MSCs on the other would improve capital mobility, but the availability of checkable assets would not fundamentally increase financial instability. In the absence of "checkability," mutual fund shares and similar assets would still be payable on demand in the sense that they can be sold rapidly by a broker or fund manager; using checks simply reduces the costs and bother. If people somehow lose faith in stocks and bonds, the inconvenience of having to call someone rather than write a check is not going to deter them from selling out.

The same potential instability exists in our current system, as the stock market crash of October 19, 1987, demonstrated. But the resiliency of the financial system, coupled with aggressive action by the Federal Reserve, averted a general panic. Such a panic is no more likely to occur if the insured checking accounts at banks are replaced by insured checking accounts offered by monetary service companies. If instability arises either under existing arrangements or with MSCs, the remedy is the same: the Federal Reserve must purchase securities and make loans available through the discount window. Under the proposal, MSCs can borrow at the discount window for purposes of purchasing commercial paper, short-term debt of unaffiliated FSCs, and other eligible assets—a convenient conduit for channeling funds to several areas of the private sector in the event of financial instability.

A central activity of monetary service companies is to provide the payment services that are currently handled by banks. MSCs will replace today's banks (and thrifts) as users of the Federal Reserve's check clearing and wire transfer systems, and they will be authorized to operate their own, private payment facilities in order to provide a smoothly functioning and safe payments system. If MSCs are going to be low-risk operations, ways must be found to reduce the payment risk that characterizes the present clearing system. Most risk can be eliminated without undue restrictions; the remainder is handled by regulation and federal insurance.

MSCs eliminate much of the prevailing credit risk. Because all checking accounts at MSCs, including what are now demand deposit accounts, pay a market rate of return, corporations will have far less incentive to turn over their accounts with such incredible speed, reducing both the volume of transactions and their risk. Furthermore, MSCs are not allowed daylight overdrafts; they are authorized to extend credit only through purchases of highly rated marketable securities. A corporation wanting to make a payment to some third party must have funds on deposit with its monetary service company before the transaction takes place.

The hazards of the payments system are reduced by these provisions, but risks remain. Within-day debit and credit positions will develop among MSCs during the course of business, exposing creditors to risk of failure by MSCs owing funds. Strong regulation and supervision of these exposures must be provided by the Federal Reserve as part of its oversight of monetary service companies. The payments system is central to the function of a modern economy and cannot be left completely in private hands.

It is appropriate to deal with the residual risk by providing federal insurance, financed by assessments on MSCs, to guarantee the finality of payment should an MSC fail. The innate safety of MSCs, coupled with Federal Reserve control of credit exposure and prohibition of daylight overdrafts, should result in low-cost insurance. By using MSCs to operate the payments system and by guaranteeing the finality of payment, it is possible to have a payments system that is safe, efficient, and stable.

Nothing in the proposal precludes FSCs from engaging in various clearing activities. FSCs can allow daylight overdrafts if they choose; they can also engage in transactions and clearing arrangements in government securities and foreign exchange. To attract business and protect themselves, FSCs will have strong incentives to self-insure much as CHIPS is currently doing. This will allow FSCs to compete in govern-

ment securities and foreign exchange markets, and their American customers will not be put at a competitive disadvantage with companies
from Europe or Asia.

Stability and Availability of Credit

It might appear that the proposal achieves safety and stability of the
monetary system by sacrificing the stability and availability of credit.
After all, checking accounts are not used to finance direct consumer
and business lending, as is currently the practice for banks and thrifts,
but rather are spun off into MSCs. The financial service companies that
provide these direct consumer and business loans are not allowed to
issue government-insured liabilities to fund their lending but must rely
on uninsured or privately insured liabilities. Less credit will be available
to consumers and business at higher cost because FSCs will not be able
to raise as much money and will have to pay higher interest rates on
liabilities not insured or guaranteed by the government. Large shifts of
funds into and out of FSCs as their fortunes wax and wane seem likely.

But the concerns are more apparent than real. Monetary service
companies will in fact extend credit directly and indirectly to business,
and indirectly to consumers, but in forms that will provide MSCs with
great protection. When MSCs purchase short-term securities issued by
finance companies, they are lending indirectly to consumers. When
MSCs purchase commercial paper, they are extending credit to business, the same kind of credit that used to be provided by banks as prime
loans. Similarly, when MSCs purchase the short-term marketable debt
issued by nonaffiliated FSCs, they are extending credit to these institutions, allowing them to fund loans to business and consumers. Although
this debt must be relatively short-term and highly rated to be eligible for
MSC purchase, it offers a large potential source of funds for well-
managed FSCs. Credit provision by MSCs is a critical element in the
financial system and illustrates why it would be poor public policy to
restrict MSCs to holdings of Treasury securities.

The financial service companies must fend for themselves. They will
not be able to attract funds from MSCs, other businesses, and the public
at large unless they manage their risks prudently. With the risks out in
the open, creditors will be inclined to monitor the activities of FSCs
much more closely and actively than they do today's banks and thrifts.
FSCs will have to disclose pertinent facts about their operations, and
creditors will insist upon and receive ratings for FSCs to allow them to
better assess risk. Well-run FSCs will have incentive to disclose their

success in order to give them a competitive advantage over less well managed institutions. The discipline demanded by creditors makes it incumbent on FSCs to protect themselves against adversity, not only by limiting the riskiness of specific loans and other activities but by adopting methods of effective diversification and retaining sufficient capital to cushion creditors. Government cease-and-desist orders and threats are replaced by penalties in the form of capital standards and interest rate premiums extracted by creditors to compensate for risk, and after some point by the unwillingness of creditors to supply funds at any price.

FSCs might find it practical and beneficial to obtain private insurance for their liabilities. To the extent that the resources of private insurers are sufficient, creditors will reduce their vigilance in monitoring FSCs. But insurers will compensate with their own monitoring and discipline, imposing capital standards and assessing risk-based premiums.

What about the stability of the system? Will not the financial services industry be vulnerable to the same kinds of panics and crises that beset banking before the New Deal reforms? The answer is no.

FSCs may be susceptible to silent runs in which otherwise healthy institutions are unable to roll over maturing debt because fear arises among their creditors. This could eventually force sharp curtailment of credit and possibly drive otherwise solvent FSCs into bankruptcy, with severe consequences for borrowers and the economy as a whole.

Several considerations militate against such calamities. The Federal Reserve is the final guarantor of liquidity to otherwise solvent institutions. The Fed can engage in open-market operations to ease general liquidity pressure, and it can use monetary service companies as conduits for channeling funds to solvent FSCs that are experiencing liquidity problems. The MSCs borrow from the Federal Reserve and use the proceeds to buy market instruments issued by financial service companies. It is important that this conduit function of MSCs not be extended beyond purchasing instruments that meet the ordinary standards for MSC investments, but the Federal Reserve can extend credit directly on an emergency basis to solvent institutions that either do not have high ratings for their money market instruments or cannot market these instruments at all.

Although the Federal Reserve is more than capable of averting liquidity crises, such crises are less likely to occur under the proposed restructuring than in today's banking system. Banks are currently able to market vast amounts of very short-term debt at favorable terms because these liabilities receive implicit government guarantees. Creditors have far too little incentive to monitor these institutions because the regulators are doing the job for them. Furthermore, they limit risk by extending credit for short periods of time. Should problems begin to surface, they can probably get their money out before a bank goes under. But the shorter the maturity of a bank's liabilities, the more quickly it can be wiped out by silent runs.

Under the proposed reforms, there is no government insurance or guarantee for the liabilities of financial service companies; institutions are allowed to fail. This will pressure FSCs to build in safeguards to protect themselves against silent runs. They will arrange for credit lines with other FSCs so that otherwise solvent institutions can obtain credit if they encounter difficulties rolling over their debt.[6] FSCs will also avoid bunching maturities for liabilities, will extend maturities of liabilities, and will hold liquid assets, all of which blunt the effect of a temporary loss of creditor confidence.

In spite of all of these natural safeguards, creditors could still conceivably lose faith in FSCs in general and demand payment when their credits mature. But the money has to go someplace, and it is highly unlikely that even during a panic FSCs' creditors will demand currency. They will shift their funds to other institutions, and one likely place is the safe accounts at monetary service companies. The MSCs will take this money and use at least part of it to purchase the securities being issued by solvent financial service companies. Some of the funds are thus recycled to where they began.

Institutions *will* fail under the proposal. Failures must be possible to encourage the market discipline that limits their scope. The pivotal point is, however, that failure of one financial service company has no particular bearing on the viability of other FSCs. With the new system functioning properly, failures will be infrequent. With recycling available from MSCs, and ultimately backed up by the Fed, systemic risk is eliminated. The failure of one FSC has no more implications for other FSCs than the failure of Montgomery Ward would have for Sears.

There is no reason to suppose that the total amount of credit extended in the economy will be affected, but the proposal will produce changes in who extends credit to whom. Large amounts of credit will flow through MSCs into market securities issued by government and private businesses. But what about financial service companies? Because FSCs will receive no government insurance or guarantees for their liabilities, they will have to pay risk premiums and maintain larger

6. This provides protection as long as only a few FSCs experience silent runs.

equity positions. Relative to today's banks and thrifts, they may find it unprofitable to hold loans in their portfolios that are capable of being securitized, such as loans to households to finance consumer durables and homes; these loans are profitable today primarily because of the federal subsidy from deposit insurance and other guarantees.

Some loans will remain profitable; after all, many finance companies currently are able to raise funds in the market without government protection and still profitably hold consumer loans despite competition from subsidized banks and thrifts. But even if FSCs find it unprofitable to hold many kinds of loans, household credit will not tighten but will be directed increasingly into the securities markets. Financial service companies will find it attractive to originate, service, and securitize mortgage and consumer loans rather than holding them in their asset portfolios. Eliminating the federal subsidy from insuring and guaranteeing non-monetary liabilities of depository institutions should accelerate the process of securitization that is already underway. Further, to the extent that FSCs can develop low-risk, short-term securities backed by consumer loans and perhaps even business loans, they will find ready purchasers in monetary service companies.

What about the kinds of business loans that cannot be securitized because they are too specialized and require too much information to be appraised by outsiders? These loans will reside in the portfolios of the financial service companies that originate them. It will continue to be profitable for FSCs to originate and hold idiosyncratic business loans, issuing liabilities to finance their positions. But at what price for borrowers? It is possible but by no means certain that the interest rates charged for these loans by FSCs will be higher than the interest rate charged by today's banks. Many banks obtain money at relatively low interest rates because their depositors and other creditors are protected. This subsidy is passed on, at least in part, to business borrowers, who pay lower interest rates because banks compete for loan customers. FSCs carrying substantial risk and little capital, unprotected by federal insurance, will have to pay higher interest rates to depositors and other creditors than would equally risky and capital-strained banks. This will lead to higher interest rates for loans.

It is not obvious, however, that the interest rates for loans held by FSCs will be higher than what had been charged by banks. The reason is that the loan portfolios of FSCs will be small compared to those of today's banks. Only loans that cannot be securitized will remain. This implies that FSCs will raise much less money than today's banks. With relatively low funding requirements and adequate equity positions,

FSCs may be able to obtain money as cheaply as banks with their huge funding requirements and low equity. Should this be the case, loan interest rates will probably not rise at all. But should FSC funding costs and loan interest rates be higher than for banks, this is simply a consequence of eliminating the costly and ineffective subsidy of federal protection proffered to today's banks and indirectly to their business borrowers. If as a matter of public policy it is deemed appropriate to subsidize these borrowers, it is far more effective to provide the subsidy directly to them rather than indirectly through protecting all the activities of the institutions that lend to them.

Another potential problem involves the fate of small banks trying to operate monetary and financial service components. These institutions can probably operate their MSCs profitably, but how can their FSCs hope to compete for funds when their liabilities are no longer insured? Those small banks kept afloat only by the subsidy of deposit insurance for all their liabilities should probably disappear, to be replaced by branches of larger institutions. But many small banks are highly profitable and stable today; they could operate profitable FSCs with low enough risk to attract funds even without insurance. Besides, the increased securitization that is bound to occur will generate income and help eliminate difficulties from inadequate diversification, which is one of the major problems faced by small institutions. Securitization will make it easier for them to acquire loans and other assets from other areas. They can originate and service many kinds of loans and sell them into pools. In short, many small institutions will survive the proposed restructuring.

The restructuring will make it more difficult for the nation's largest banks to compete in certain international credit markets. Large banks in all countries currently enjoy protection from their governments. This has allowed them to raise vast sums in domestic and international money markets. Competition among these banks has pushed down interest rates on their loans to major corporations and governments to the point that this business is barely profitable. This is not surprising because these borrowers have access to international securities markets; banks have little to offer and earn little as a result. Some U.S. banks have reduced their activities in these low-margin international loan markets, but others remain. When the nonmonetary liabilities of American banks are no longer protected, holders of their negotiable CDs and Euroaccounts will switch to protected foreign banks unless compensated for the greater risk with higher interest rates from U.S. banks. With American banks paying higher interest rates for their liabilities than foreign banks, U.S. banks will find it difficult, if not impossible, to compete with their foreign counterparts for low-margin international loans.

The competitiveness of U.S. banks in low-margin international credit markets is likely to be reduced. But this decline in American "competitiveness" should not be lamented. Large banks all over the world are granting loans whose return does not justify the risk. This is possible because their governments stand behind their banks. That other countries continue this destructive and ultimately costly practice is no justification for the United States to do so.

It would be desirable for all major nations to stop protecting the nonmonetary liabilities of their banks, but there is no need to await cooperation. The United States will benefit from acting unilaterally and other countries will discover, as we have, that their protective measures are counterproductive. Such discovery is underway. For example, Japanese banks—the largest in the world—are experiencing poor earnings and face the chance of suffering major losses, exposing their government to substantial expense.

The Transition: Getting from Here to There

Formulating a transition to the proposed new financial structure is in some respects as important as the proposal; the new structure represents too great a departure for immediate implementation. Radical departures from the *status quo* only occur when there is a crisis, as in 1933, and then the pressure of events rather than careful planning conditions the results.

The transition involves the introduction of several reforms discussed at the end of chapter 4. A first step is to impose coinsurance, in which the costs of bank failures are shared between the FDIC and large, uninsured depositors.[7] The costs include losses from FDIC payouts when banks are closed and the expenses of arranging takeovers. The potential loss for large depositors is initially small—they could lose a maximum of 10 percent of the principal and interest owed to them by a failed bank.[8] This risk exposure is low enough to avoid a massive outcry from large depositors while inducing them to extract interest rate premiums and increased equity positions from risky banks.

7. Unsecured loans extended by banks are also covered by coinsurance.
8. Large depositors at small banks will actually enjoy a reduction in their risk exposure during the transition because under existing practices the FDIC may not bail them out completely as it does their counterparts at large banks that fail.

All types of deposits currently covered by insurance are to continue to enjoy protection, but the insurance limit is to be on a per depositor basis—initially retained at $100,000—and rigorously enforced; any balances in excess of the limit are to be subject to coinsurance. Checking accounts are the exception. For them, insurance is to be extended beyond the limit applied to other accounts provided that a bank secures balances in a checking account in excess of that limit by low-risk, short-term market securities of the type to be allowed for MSCs.[9] Institutions that set up separately capitalized MSCs are to have the checking accounts in these companies insured without limit. MSCs are to be allowed to pay interest on their business accounts, giving businesses a powerful motive to shift funds out of their noninterest-bearing checking accounts at banks into MSCs.

The transition also entails limiting the use of brokered deposits as a method for large banks to replace liabilities subject to coinsurance with insured accounts, and for large depositors to achieve full insurance protection by spreading accounts across a number of banks. Although the initial $100,000 limit is for all bank accounts other than secured checking accounts, it is to be set strictly on a per depositor basis. For reasons explained in chapter 4, depositors can have insured accounts in a maximum of five banks that must be identified before failure. Also for reasons explained earlier, depositors with insured accounts in a bank that fails receive a charge against their $100,000 insurance quota equal to the amount of insured money they have in that bank and earn back their full quota over five years.

Over time, the extent of coinsurance will be increased gradually until accounts with balances in excess of the insurance limit—except for secured checking accounts and accounts at MSCs—are completely at risk. The insurance limit is also gradually reduced to zero. At that point, secured checking accounts and MSC liabilities will be the only insured accounts at banks (and thrifts). The process can be spread out over a decade or more, but ultimately depositors and other creditors of banks will assume responsibility for all the principal and interest owed them. The risk exposure for the FDIC is reduced commensurately.

The proposed transition also involves exploiting and gradually altering the holding company structure for banks to encourage division of activities between MSCs and FSCs.[10] The essential first step is to attain corporate separateness between banks and all other elements of their

9. Technically, checking accounts are to include all transactions accounts as presently defined by the Federal Reserve for purposes of imposing reserve requirements.
10. The steps that follow are also to be applied to S&L holding companies.

holding companies. This is done by ending the Federal Reserve's regulation of parent holding companies and their nonbank affiliates, including elimination of capital requirements for holding companies and of the stricture that parent companies and nonbank affiliates serve as sources of strength for affiliated banks. Further, creditors of parent companies and nonbank affiliates are to be at risk—the FDIC is to expend no funds in their behalf—and are not to be responsible for the obligations of banking affiliates or their subsidiaries. In order that banks be protected against other constituents of these holding companies, the Federal Reserve is to continue to police transactions between banks and these constituents, and penalties are to be increased for violations of sections 23A and 23B of the Federal Reserve Act, including the imposition of criminal penalties for willful violation of the limits on these transactions.[11]

With corporate separateness firmly in place, bank holding companies are to be gradually granted new powers like full securities activities and the ability to offer general forms of insurance, but these activities must be conducted by nonbank subsidiaries and not by banks. The new subsidiaries are not to be regulated by the Federal Reserve or any other banking regulator. They are treated just as securities firms and insurance companies are treated today.[12] The new subsidiaries are not covered by the federal safety net, so their creditors are at risk. By law these creditors are to have no claim on the bank or banks in the holding company. As these changes take place, existing securities firms and insurance companies are allowed to acquire or establish banks through bank holding companies. These firms also receive no protection from the safety net, and their creditors have no claim on the banks in the holding companies.

Along with these changes, banks and bank holding companies are to receive increasing incentives to shift existing nonmonetary activities into unprotected and unregulated holding company subsidiaries which are allowed to share facilities and personnel with monetary activities. Nonmonetary business conducted by the regulated and protected part of banks (and thrifts) and their subsidiaries are to be subjected over time to substantial and rising capital requirements issued by their primary regulator. These requirements can be avoided by shifting the activities into separate, unregulated, and unprotected holding company

11. Limits on credit extensions in section 23A are to be extended to cover daylight overdrafts granted by banks to their nonbank affiliates or parent companies.
12. They are regulated by the SEC and state insurance agencies, respectively.

subsidiaries. By gradually raising the capital requirements to onerous levels, activities not conducted by monetary service companies are forced out of the regulated and protected part of existing banks. At some point—perhaps as long as a decade after the process begins— holding companies are required to shift any remaining nonmonetary service activities to unprotected and unregulated subsidiaries. Monetary and financial services become functionally separated within their banks and their holding company structures.

Over time, banks (and thrifts) will be subjected to increasing market discipline, and a growing number of financial dealings will be conducted by holding company subsidiaries that do not enjoy government protection and are not under the jurisdiction of the banking regulators. Progress may be relatively slow and orderly, allowing ample opportunity for adjustment and verification that monetary and credit stability is working. The transition can be slowed down or speeded up as conditions warrant. When the transition is complete, owners of financial service companies can own what have become monetary service companies, but these companies are tightly regulated, notably with ironclad restrictions on financial transactions with affiliates and owners. By this time, there is nothing left for the banking regulators to do. The bank and thrift regulatory agencies are then eliminated, with the regulation and federal insurance of MSCs consolidated in the Federal Reserve.

The banking regulators have a great deal to do during the transition, however. They are to improve supervisory techniques, including the use of market accounting as a method of providing earlier warning that banks may be in trouble, and they are to move more quickly to close failed banks or arrange takeovers of the banks' activities. Pressures from large depositors and other creditors who are increasingly at risk and want to limit their losses will also help speed detection of failing banks.

The banking regulators are also obliged to help the transition along. It is unlikely that regulators will take the initiative in promoting a smooth transition toward elimination of their jobs. Strong leadership by both Congress and the executive branch will be required to develop clear marching orders for the regulators through law and administrative procedure. The transition involves more than just increasing capital requirements for nonmonetary activities of banks. Officials are to counsel and generally aid smaller institutions in developing methods of securitizing their assets and marketing their liabilities. With the banking regulators playing a positive role, the transition can be relatively smooth and orderly.

The purpose of this book has been to argue that the appropriate role of public policy is to regulate and protect the monetary activities that have historically been conducted by banks. This can be done effectively by invoking and enforcing the doctrine of corporate separateness for monetary service activities within banks and financial conglomerates. Other financial services can be left largely to the market without the heavy hand of government regulation and without government protection of individual financial service firms. The Federal Reserve's open-market operations and activities as lender of last resort provide adequate protection against instability in the credit markets.

It is counterproductive and dangerous to continue to regulate and protect an increasing array of financial services. Unless this policy is reversed, the problems that the banking regulators and the deposit insurance agency face will worsen. Plans should be laid now to define appropriate policies for the future. I hope this volume has contributed to that process.

Selected References

Chapter 2: Some Fundamentals

Bernanke, B. "Nonmonetary Effects of the Financial Crisis in Propagation of the Great Depression." *American Economic Review,* June 1983.

Bernanke, B., and M. Gertler. "Agency Costs, Net Worth, and Business Fluctuations." *American Economic Review,* March 1989.

Chan, Y., and A. Thaker. "Collateral and Competitive Equilibria with Moral Hazard and Private Information." *Journal of Finance,* June 1987.

Diamond, D., and P. Dybvig. "Bank Runs, Deposit Insurance, and Liquidity." *Journal of Political Economy,* June 1983.

Fama, E. "Banking in the Theory of Finance." *Journal of Monetary Economics,* January 1980.

Gorton, G. "Bank Suspension of Convertibility." *Journal of Monetary Economics,* March 1985.

Leland, H., and D. Pyle. "Information Asymmetries, Financial Structure, and Financial Intermediation." *Journal of Finance,* May 1977.

Smith, B. "Private Information, Deposit Interest Rates, and the Stability of the Banking System." *Journal of Monetary Economics,* November 1984.

Stiglitz, J. "Credit Markets and the Control of Capital." *Journal of Money, Credit and Banking,* May 1985.

Stiglitz, J., and A. Weiss. "Credit Rationing in Markets with Imperfect Information." *American Economic Review,* June 1981.

153

Williamson, S. "Costly Monitoring, Financial Intermediation, and Equilibrium Credit Rationing." *Journal of Monetary Economics,* September 1986.

―――. "Recent Developments in Modeling Financial Intermediation." Federal Reserve Bank of Minneapolis, *Quarterly Review,* Summer 1987.

Chapter 3: The Evolution of Banking in the United States

Cagan, P. "The First Fifty Years of the National Banking System: An Appraisal." In D. Carsen, ed., *Banking and Monetary Studies.* Homewood, Ill.: Irwin, 1963.

Cooper, K., and D. Fraser. *Bank Deregulation and the New Competition in Financial Services.* Cambridge, Mass: Ballinger, 1986.

Cox, E. "The Changing Role of Banks in the Financial Services Industry." In Cox et al., *The Bank Director's Handbook,* 2d ed. Dover, Mass.: Auburn House, 1986.

Cumming, C. "The Economics of Securitization." Federal Reserve Bank of New York, *Quarterly Review,* Autumn 1987.

Friedman, M., and A. Schwartz. *A Monetary History of the United States, 1867–1960.* Princeton, N.J.: Princeton University Press, 1963.

Glassman, C. "U.S. Financial Institutions in a World Market." In C. Glassman, J. Pierce, R. Karmel, and J. LaFalce, *Regulating the New Financial Services Industry.* Washington, D.C.: Center for National Policy Press, 1988.

Golembe, C. "The Deposit Insurance Legislation of 1933." *Political Science Quarterly,* June 1960.

Goodfriend, M. "Eurodollars." In *Instruments of the Money Market.* Richmond, Va.: Federal Reserve Bank of Richmond, 1986.

Gorton, G., and D. Mullineaux. "The Joint Production of Confidence: Endogenous Regulation and Nineteenth-Century Commercial-Bank Clearing Houses." *Journal of Money, Credit, and Banking,* November 1987.

Guttentag, J., and R. Herring. *The Current Crisis in International Lending.* Washington, D.C.: Brookings Institution, 1985.

Hammond, B. "Banking before the Civil War." In D. Carsen, ed., *Banking and Monetary Studies.* Homewood, Ill.: Irwin, 1963.

Kaufman, G. "The Truth about Bank Runs." In C. England and T. Huertes, eds., *The Financial Services Revolution.* Boston, Mass.: Kluwer Academic Publishers, 1988.

Klebaner, B. *Commercial Banking in the United States: A History.* Hinsdale, Ill.: Dryden Press, 1974.

Kwast, M., ed. *Financial Futures and Options in the U.S. Economy.* Study by the Staff of the Federal Reserve System, Washington, D.C., December 1986.

Lee, S., and P. Passell. *A New Economic View of American History.* New York: W. W. Norton, 1979, chapter 6.

Litan, R. *What Should Banks Do?* Washington, D.C.: Brookings Institution, 1987.

Makin, J. *The Global Debt Crisis.* New York: Basic Books, 1984.

Pierce, J. *Monetary and Financial Economics*. New York: John Wiley and Sons, 1984.

Pierce, J., and S. Chase. *Management of Bank Risk*. Washington, D.C.: Association of Reserve City Bankers, 1988.

Platt, R., ed. *Controlling Interest Rate Risk*. New York: John Wiley and Sons, 1986.

Pozdena, R. "Mortgage Securitization and REMICs." Federal Reserve Bank of San Francisco, *Weekly Letter*, May 8, 1987.

Sachs, J., ed. *Developing Country Debt and the World Economy*. Chicago: University of Chicago Press, 1988.

Schlesinger, A., Jr. *The Age of Jackson*. Boston: Little, Brown, 1946.

———. *The Coming of the New Deal*. Boston: Houghton Mifflin, 1958.

———. *The Crisis of the Old Order, 1919–1933*. Boston: Houghton Mifflin, 1957.

Schwartz, A. "Real and Pseudo-Financial Crises." In F. Capie and G. E. Wood, eds., *Financial Crises and the World Banking System*. New York: St. Martin's Press, 1986.

Stigum, M. *The Money Market: Myth, Reality, and Practice*. Homewood, Ill.: Dow Jones-Irwin, 1978.

Studenski, P., and H. Kross. *Financial History of the United States*, 2d ed. New York: McGraw-Hill, 1963.

U.S. Senate Committee on Banking and Currency. *Federal Banking Law and Reports 1780–1912*. Washington, D.C.: Government Printing Office, 1963.

Whittaker, J. "Interest Rate Swaps: Risk and Regulation." Federal Reserve Bank of Kansas City, *Economic Review*, March 1987.

Chapter 4: Bank Regulation and the Federal Safety Net

American Bankers Association. *Federal Deposit Insurance: A Program for Reform*. Washington, D.C.: American Bankers Association, March 1990.

Association of Reserve City Bankers. *Risks in the Electronic Payments System*. Washington, D.C.: Association of Reserve City Bankers, 1983.

Balderston, F. *Thrifts in Crisis*. Cambridge, Mass.: Ballinger, 1985.

Brookings Institution. *Blue Print for Restructuring America's Financial Institutions*. Washington, D.C.: Brookings Institution, 1989.

Board of Governors of the Federal Reserve System. *Capital Adequacy Guidelines*. Washington, D.C.: Federal Reserve, March 1989.

———. "Daylight Overdrafts and Payment System Risk." *Federal Reserve Bulletin*, November 1987.

Chase, S. "Insulating Banks from Risks Run by Nonbank Affiliates." Washington, D.C.: Chase, Laub, October 1987.

Feldstein, M. "Latin America's Debt: Muddling Through Can Be Just Fine." *Economist*, June 27, 1987.

Gelfand, M., and D. Lindsey. "The Simple Microanalytics of Payments System Risk." Board of Governors of the Federal Reserve System, *Finance and Economics Discussion Series,* Washington, D.C., March 1989.

Kane, E. "Appearances and Reality in Deposit Insurance: A Case for Reform." *Journal of Banking and Finance,* June 1986.

————. "Dangers of Capital Forbearance: The Case of the FSLIC and 'Zombie' S&Ls." *Contemporary Policy Issues.* Western Economic Association, Long Beach, Calif., January 1987.

————. *The Gathering Crisis in Federal Deposit Insurance.* Cambridge, Mass.: MIT Press, 1985.

Kareken, J. "Federal Bank Regulatory Policy: A Description and Some Observations." *Journal of Business,* January 1986.

Lash, N. *Banking Laws and Regulation.* Englewood Cliffs, N.J.: Prentice-Hall, 1987.

Moulton, J. "New Guidelines for Bank Capital: An Attempt to Reflect Risk." Federal Reserve Bank of Philadelphia, *Business Review,* July–August 1987.

Neuberger, J. "FIRREA and Deposit Insurance Reform." Federal Reserve Bank of San Francisco, *Weekly Letter,* December 1, 1989.

Pierce, J., and S. Chase. *Management of Bank Risk.* Washington, D.C.: Association of Reserve City Bankers, 1988.

Pyle, D. "Capital Regulation and Deposit Insurance." *Journal of Banking and Finance,* June 1986.

U.S. House of Representatives. *Financial Institutions Reform, Recovery, and Enforcement Act of 1989.* Washington, D.C.: Government Printing Office, August 4, 1989.

U.S. House of Representatives, Committee on Government Operations, "Modernization of the Financial Services Industry: A Plan for Capital Mobility within a Framework of Safe and Sound Banking." Sixteenth Report of the Committee on Government Operations, Washington, D.C., September 30, 1987.

Van Hoose, D., and G. Sellon. "Daylight Overdrafts, Payments System Risk, and Public Policy." Federal Reserve Bank of Kansas City, *Economic Review,* September–October 1989.

Walter, I. "Country Risk, Portfolio Decisions and Regulation in International Bank Lending." *Journal of Banking and Finance,* March 1981.

Chapter 5: A New Approach

Brookings Institution. *Blue Print for Restructuring America's Financial Institutions.* Washington, D.C.: Brookings Institution, 1989.

Chase, S. "Insulating Banks from Risks Run by Nonbank Affiliates." *American Bankers Association,* Washington, D.C., 1987.

Cooper, K., and D. Fraser. *Banking Deregulation and the New Competition in Financial Services.* Cambridge, Mass.: Ballinger, 1986.

Federal Reserve Bank of Kansas City. Restructuring the Financial System: A Symposium. Kansas City, Mo., 1987.

Fraser, D., and J. Kolari. *The Future of Small Banks in a Deregulated Environment.* Cambridge, Mass.: Ballinger, 1985.

Haraf, W., and R. Kushmeider, eds. *Restructuring Banking and Financial Services in America.* Washington, D.C.: American Enterprise Institute, 1988.

Litan, R. *What Should Banks Do?* Washington, D.C.: Brookings Institution, 1987.

Pierce, J. "Financial Reform in the United States and the Financial System of the Future." In *Financial Innovation and Monetary Policy: Asia and the West; Proceedings of the Second International Conference Held by the Bank of Japan,* ed. Y. Suzuki and H. Yomo. Tokyo: University of Tokyo Press, 1986.

———. "Integrating Banking and Other Financial Services." In C. Glassman, J. Pierce, R. Karmel, and J. LaFalce, *Regulating the New Financial Services Industry.* Washington, D.C.: Center for National Policy Press, 1988.

———. "Can Banks Be Isolated from Nonbank Affiliates?" In *Governing Banking's Future,* ed. Catherine England. Boston, Mass.: Kluwer Academic Publishers, 1991.

U.S. House of Representatives, Committee on Government Operations. "Modernization of the Financial Services Industry: A Plan for Capital Mobility within a Framework of Safe and Sound Banking." Sixteenth Report of the Committee on Government Operations, Washington, D.C., September 30, 1987.

Walter, E., ed. *Deregulating Wall Street.* New York: John Wiley and Sons, 1985.

Index